EVERY CONGREGATION
Needs a Little
CONFLICT

**The Columbia Partnership Leadership Series
from Chalice Press**

www.chalicepress.com
www.thecolumbiapartnership.org

EVERY
CONGREGATION
Needs a Little
CONFLICT

GEORGE W. BULLARD JR.

CHALICE
P R E S S

ST. LOUIS, MISSOURI

All Scripture, unless otherwise marked, is taken from the *NEW AMERICAN STANDARD BIBLE* ®, © Copyright The Lockman Foundation 1960, 1962, 1963, 1968, 1971, 1972, 1973, 1975, 1977, 1995. Used by permission.

Cover image: Elizabeth Wright, using images from Fotosearch and Digital Stock
Cover and interior design: Elizabeth Wright

Visit Chalice Press on the World Wide Web at
www.chalicepress.com

10 9 8 7 6 5 4 3 2 1   08   09   10   11   12   13

Library of Congress Cataloging-in-Publication Data

Bullard, George, 1950-
Every congregation needs a little conflict / by George W. Bullard Jr.
    p. cm.
ISBN 978-0-8272-0819-3
    1. Church controversies. I. Title.
BV652.9.B85 2008
250—dc22   2007046280

Printed in the United States of America

Contents

Editor's Foreword

Inspiration and Wisdom for Twenty-First–Century Christian Leaders

You have chosen wisely in deciding to study and learn from a book published in **The Columbia Partnership Leadership Series** with Chalice Press. We publish for

- Congregational leaders who desire to serve with greater faithfulness, effectiveness, and innovation.
- Christian ministers who seek to pursue and sustain excellence in ministry service.
- Members of congregations who desire to reach their full kingdom potential.
- Christian leaders who desire to use a coach approach in their ministry.
- Denominational and parachurch leaders who want to come alongside affiliated congregations in a servant leadership role.
- Consultants and coaches who desire to increase their learning concerning the congregations and Christian leaders they serve.

The Columbia Partnership Leadership Series is an inspiration- and wisdom-sharing vehicle of The Columbia Partnership, a community of Christian leaders who are seeking to transform the capacity of the North American Protestant church to pursue and sustain vital Christ-centered ministry. You can connect with us at www.TheColumbiaPartnership.org.

Primarily serving congregations, denominations, educational institutions, leadership development programs, and parachurch organizations, the Partnership also seeks to connect with individuals, businesses, and other organizations seeking a Christ-centered spiritual focus.

We welcome your comments on these books, and we welcome your suggestions for new subject areas and authors we ought to consider.

George W. Bullard Jr., Senior Editor
GBullard@TheColumbiaPartnership.org

The Columbia Partnership,
905 Hwy 321 NW, Suite 331, Hickory, NC 28601
Voice: 866.966.4TCP, www.TheColumbiaPartnership.org

Introduction

Welcome to a book on the number one growth industry for Christian congregations: conflict. The growth rate is exponential. The product life cycle is still in ascendancy and shows no signs of peaking. Those who deal in conflict resolution, mediation, and management are busy people.

Books about conflict are a necessary evil. This is another one. I wish it did not have to be written. But this is an extremely important book and will apply to many more congregations than we would like to imagine.

Here is the good news. Every congregation needs a little conflict. Conflict is actually a great thing for congregations if it comes in small doses. In large doses it can be devastating to Christian ministry, and to the people it impacts. Many things are good in small doses. Coffee, chocolate, and medicines of various kinds come to mind. In large doses medical science warns us they are all more harmful than good.

My History with Conflict

My personal history with conflict is checkered. Early in my ministry I was extremely confrontational, quick-tempered, and did not handle conflict well when I was one of the primary persons involved in the conflict. Some people who know me now may still wonder about my ability to handle what is known as two-party conflict. This is conflict in which I am personally involved as one of the participants in the conflict.

I was a social activist on various issues thirty to forty years ago. I would strongly proclaim my positions and not be open to negotiation with people who did not see things my way. For those who remember this name, Saul Alinsky was my social activism hero. In college I did an independent study on French syndicalism as a radical labor movement and its call for the general strike by all workers. I was also interested in dialectical materialism and its impact on the structure of communism. These were all part of my college rebellion years. In reality I was much more talk than action. I am a much more plain and boring guy now.

Then in my seminary pastorate I pursued my youth minister across town to a meeting he was attending. Why? Because I received a report of something foolish he had done—something quite different from what I had instructed him to do. This was the same congregation in which I had to stand between two deacons in the middle of our monthly meeting as they had their fists cocked to take punches at each other. Lucky for me neither threw a punch.

In my early years as a consultant on strategic issues with congregations, I badly handled conflict going on in the congregation in which I had grown up. I acted in a destructive rather than constructive way toward the pastor. I was impatient with what I interpreted as incompetence. I still am, and it gets me in trouble from time to time. Some measure of tolerance has come with age, but an edge is still there.

Unfortunately, many congregational and denominational situations have a measure of conflict in them. Often an intervention or change process will bring to the surface issues of conflict that congregations do not want to engage. Early in my years as a consultant I encountered a lot of situations in which congregations would not acknowledge that one of their key issues was conflict.

I asked one of my mentors what he did when he was consulting with congregations in which some issue of conflict arose for which he had no warning. He said he did two things. First, he confronted the pastor for lying to him. He always asks up front, "Is this is a conflict situation?" because he never goes into a conflicted congregation. Second, he got an early flight home.

My Leadership in Conflict Ministry

More than twenty-five years ago, I was on the national missions staff for my denomination. Our area of work was considering the training needs of local denominational leaders. We determined that, in many areas where training was needed, no one inside or outside our denomination adequately understood both the training needed and the context of local denominational organizations.

We decided each of us would choose one of the top priority areas and seek training ourselves to become experts who could deliver training to our leaders with an understanding of the context. I chose conflict. I knew I had so much to learn in this area. I was hoping I could be a learner while helping others to learn.

It was a great choice. It was a great help to me in my ministry. It opened opportunities to provide training for many congregational and denominational leaders. In later years it has been very useful to me in my consulting and coaching roles with numerous congregations and denominations in conflict.

For more than twenty-five years I have worked in the areas of research, writing, teaching, consulting, and coaching in the processes being written about in this book. The material behind this book has been used throughout North America among dozens of denominations.

From 1983 through 1993 I conducted weeklong training at national conference centers for three levels of conflict ministry and management training: awareness training, advanced skills training, and consultant training. More than 500 congregational and denominational leaders participated in one or more of these levels of training.

I have consulted with hundreds of congregations on issues of conflict, and used information, knowledge, and wisdom about conflict in consultation with congregations and denominational organizations. I have consulted with dozens of congregations and denominations in which the specific issue that brought me there was an unhealthy intensity of conflict.

Particularly for the period of 1989 through 1995 I was seen as the *hired gun* who went into some severely conflicted congregations up and down the East Coast in attempts to meaningfully engage their conflicts with a compelling style that would guarantee something significant would happen as a result of each encounter. Beginning in 1996 I focused my conflict management efforts on helping denominational organizations to deal with their conflict situations.

The Focus of This Book

The purpose of this book is to help congregational, denominational, and parachurch leadership empower congregations throughout various intensities of conflict, and to use conflict in a healthy manner to deal with the issues confronting congregations.

My primary focus is to suggest that every congregation needs a little conflict so it can learn how to deal with healthy conflict and use it as an empowerment vehicle. A congregation can also use the skills and habits it develops at lower intensities of conflict to see its way through unhealthy, high intensities of conflict.

People who read this book should understand the seven intensities of conflict, how to assess their congregations according to these intensities, how to educate their congregations through healthy processes of decision-making at lower intensities of conflict, how and when to bring in outside assistance, and how to confront dysfunctional and destructive conflict.

I have written this book because (1) most of the approaches to congregation conflict I observe deal inadequately and indecisively with the issues of conflict compared to what it takes to appropriately engage conflict; (2) I desire to share my experience in conflict ministry, mediation, and management with congregations; (3) too many congregations and their leadership do not understand how to handle decision-making and cultural adjustments in their congregations, and thus their leadership often escalates conflict; (4) many denominational leaders indicate they spend an increasing amount of their time dealing with issues of conflict within and between congregations and seem burdened by the this without knowing how to get out of the situation; and (5) I believe my experience and the effectiveness of my conflict management consultations give me something new and effective to contribute to the conflict ministry, mediation, and management processes.

This book is not just another process for dealing with congregational conflict. It is new in that it (1) speaks to a model and approach that has been effective in many congregations; (2) speaks to a model that has been tested in congregations for almost twenty years and about which there has not been many books written, and (3) focuses on capacity building in congregations so that learning what works in the midst of conflict and how to hardwire new learnings into the congregation are strong components of the process recommended. The seven intensities of conflict used in this book are built on five levels of conflict developed more than twenty years ago by Speed Leas, of the Alban Institute in the Washington, D.C. area (www.Alban.org). I have built on his material for twenty-five years to the point that I have taken it to a different, but related, dimension of understanding and application. It may or may not be an improvement. You will need to judge.

Some years ago Speed and I spent an evening in dialogue about my seven intensities, and he agreed they were faithful to his five levels. I pray it honors his groundbreaking work that has influenced so many congregations and their leaders. One significant difference, though, in our work is that many of Speed's consultations were in mainline denominations, and most of mine have been in evangelical denominations.

This book will help pastors, staff ministers, lay leaders, denomination servants, parachurch leaders, and consultants or coaches understand the type of conflict they might experience in their congregation, how to use conflict as a positive force for transition and change, and how to handle unhealthy conflict that might arise. It can be used for personal learning; for training classes within congregations; for training classes by denominational organizations; in college, Bible institute, and seminary classes; and in seminars conducted by myself and my ministry colleagues with The Columbia Partnership at www.TheColumbiaPartnership.org.

What Can You Learn from This Book?

Under the umbrella concept that every congregation needs a little conflict, you can learn at least seven things from this book.

1. You can learn about the intensities of conflict and how to assess at which intensity a given situation is being played out.
2. You can gain information that will help you educate participants in your congregation concerning conflict so they do not unnecessarily escalate conflict because they do not understand it and are afraid of it. Too many congregational leaders are conflict illiterate.
3. You can learn how to use conflict as an empowering force at lower intensities of conflict and to handle it appropriately before it becomes a destructive force at higher intensities of conflict.
4. Discovery of your personal conflict management styles will be a key learning.
5. Learning when you need to call in outside assistance with conflict can impact how well or how badly conflict situations in which you are involved are handled.
6. Stories and illustrations can give you a new appreciation for people and the issues that impact the conflict.
7. I hope you can learn earlier than I did in life how to handle appropriately conflict that seems to come at you from out of nowhere, and not to overreact to it, but to learn how to disagree with people without being disagreeable.

Perhaps the most important learnings will be those discoveries you have when the material informs you, and God inspires you to new insights surrounding conflict.

Reading This Book

Each chapter of this book has an organizational logic or outline that begins with a short *Executive Summary* of what is the key content of each chapter. This is followed by the main text. Somewhere near the middle of the main text, we will take a *Coaching Break*, where a series of questions and issues will be proposed to you as your gaze out the window and think about what has been shared to that point.

Near the end of the text for each chapter is a section called *Coaching Insights* that focuses on the various learnings from that chapter, and offers questions for the reader to ponder as he or she considers applications for the information and knowledge shared in the chapter. Each chapter closes with an opportunity for *Personal Reflections* on the material presented in the chapter; dialogue around actions you need to take about your life, ministry, and/or congregation on material presented in the chapter; and the challenge to be held accountable for these actions.

People Who Helped Make This Book Possible

I want to express my appreciation to Speed Leas for being a tremendous, positive influence in my life in the area of conflict ministry and management. He has been a wonderful teacher and mentor over the years. My most concentrated years with him were between 1981 and 1985, but every several years since then we still have had the opportunity to connect.

I also appreciate the team of Larry McSwain and Bill Treadwell for their book *Conflict Ministry in the Church* (Broadman Press, 1981) that they wrote a couple of decades ago, for their personal mentoring of me in the area of conflict and so many other areas, for their assistance with training events I organized beginning more than twenty years ago, and for the collegial relationship I enjoyed with them in the midst of my consultations with congregations in severe conflict. I really miss Bill's counsel, as he is now experiencing the joys of eternity and probably advising heavenly hosts on relationships among various saints and sinners.

COACHING INSIGHTS

As you weave your way through this book, it is important to understand your beginning point. Consider these issues.

■ What is your history and pattern of involvement in conflict situations? Are you a helpful presence or a hurtful presence? Do you tend to be one of the persons often involved in conflict situations, one who avoids conflict, or one who comes alongside those in conflict as a support person to them or a mediator of the conflict?

■ What do you know about conflict? Have you sought to study its positive contribution to the spiritual strategic journey of a congregation? What are you doing to learn how to handle conflict at lower intensities so you will be better prepared to handle conflict at higher intensities?

■ What do you know about your personal response to conflict? How do you handle and express your emotions at various intensities of conflict? When is the point when you move from focusing on principles to focusing on people, from focusing on *everyone* winning to focusing on *you* winning?

PERSONAL REFLECTIONS

Your Reflections: What are your reflections on the material presented in this introduction?

_____

_____

_____

_____

Your Actions: What actions do you need to take about your life, ministry, and/or congregation based on the material presented in this introduction?

_____

_____

_____

_____

Your Accountability: How and by whom do you want to be held accountable for taking these actions?

_____

_____

_____

_____

1

The Necessity of Conflict in Congregations

EXECUTIVE SUMMARY

The purpose of this chapter is to provide an overview of the processes for helping a congregation define and understand the presence of conflict. One focus will be on the necessity of conflict in the Christian experience, and its necessity in the community of believers known as a congregation. The seven intensities of conflict will be introduced.

Every Congregation Needs a Little Conflict

Every congregation needs a little conflict. Why? Because congregations without conflict are dead or dying. Conflict is a typical, common component of life. A byproduct of conflict is energy and passion. Conflict forces decisions and action. Every congregation needs a little conflict, or a healthy intensity of conflict for at least the following seven reasons.

1. Congregations without a healthy intensity of conflict do not have passion around their mission, purpose, and vision. They are directionless. They have little or no ownership of their spiritual strategic journey. Congregations with a healthy intensity of conflict must address their mission, purpose, and

vision. They must clarify their identity and direction or be forced into an unhealthy conflict situation.

2. Congregations without a healthy intensity of conflict do not have clear beliefs and core values. They refuse to clearly define their beliefs and values, perhaps because they are afraid of conflict. When congregations experience healthy conflict, one way they interact with it is to seek to bring clarity to beliefs and values.

3. Congregations without a healthy intensity of conflict function in an avoidance lifestyle. They are afraid to address issues because they are concerned about experiencing conflict. As a result, they are captivated by an immature emotional culture in which the tough decisions of life cannot be addressed except through simple answers, indoctrination, and blind loyalty.

4. Congregations without a healthy intensity of conflict make shallow decisions that come from a group-think mentality. The need exists to agree, particularly with leaders. Harmony and homogeneity are promoted rather than diversity and innovation. I know, I know. You are thinking, "Harmony is a bad thing?" Yes, especially when it is achieved at the expense of in-depth spiritual and strategic thinking and action.

5. Congregations without a healthy intensity of conflict do not have the opportunity to learn how to handle decision-making around complex issues and thus how to handle transitional and unhealthy conflict when it is experienced. These congregations end up being emotionally immature in decision-making and so inexperienced in complex decision-making that they do not know how to handle tough challenges that come their way.

6. Congregations without a healthy intensity of conflict do not learn how to keep conflict from escalating to an unhealthy intensity. Because they do not know how—or refuse—to deal with healthy intensities of conflict, significant conflict situations get out of hand too quickly.

7. Congregations without a healthy intensity of conflict do not take many risks because they are afraid taking risks will create conflict they cannot handle. They are unable to reach their full Kingdom potential. They focus too much on conflict avoidance. They ultimately plateau, decline, and perhaps die.

Is it ever possible for congregations to benefit from an *unhealthy* intensity of conflict? Yes, but it depends. I would never want to suggest that an unhealthy intensity of conflict is a good thing for congregations. But from my experience, I would go so far as to say God can bring forth good things from an unhealthy intensity of conflict. But I would not say God causes conflict to bring forth good things.

In all except the most extreme situations of life, I would never want to be party to generating an unhealthy intensity of conflict just so something good might happen on the other end. The risks are far too great, and the pain that occurs during an unhealthy intensity of conflict is far too unloving.

COACHING BREAK

✔ Gaze out the window for a minute. Ponder the situation of your congregation. What images come to mind?

✔ What are some of the ways in which you experience conflict in your congregation as good and helpful? What would be the result if good and helpful conflict were not present in your congregation?

✔ What is your congregation doing to learn how to proactively deal with the conflict that is typical and natural for any congregation? What are the consequences of not learning how to deal with typical and natural conflict?

Congregational Conflict Is Necessary and Healthy

Simply defined, conflict is the struggle of two objects seeking to occupy the same space at the same time. Purposes, objectives, or goals can be in conflict among individuals, groups, or organizations. Conflict is not an objective fact; it is a subjective experience. In another sense, conflict begins as a neutral value. People interpret conflict as positive or negative, healthy or unhealthy. The value assigned to conflict will help determine whether the conflict can be resolved or must be managed.

Conflict can occur at the intrapersonal level, the interpersonal level, the inter-group or sub-system level, and at the organism, organization, or system-wide level

Conflict can be expressed in attitudes, emotions, through communication, or in substantive issues. Much conflict lacks significant substantive issues. Antagonists who promote unhealthy conflict as righteousness should be confronted and dealt with before they destroy churches. Churches that have been severely wounded need to be loved and taught a pattern of interpersonal relationship that prevents them from returning to unhealthy patterns of conflict.

Conflict is all around us. Think about the simple act of clapping your hands. If done as an act of praise it is a healthy action. If done to assume authority by clapping hard to get the attention of people around you, it moves into the grey area. If done to indicate you intend to slap or hit someone, it is an unhealthy action. However, the action of bringing your hands together is the same in each incident. The force and intent are different.

Conflict can be healthy. Consider a violin. This instrument is capable of producing beautiful music as a result of appropriate tension on the strings, and artful drawing of the bow across the strings. Conflict also can be unhealthy. Too much tension on the violin strings will break them, or untalented drawing of the bow across the strings will produce painful noise rather than beautiful music.

Just as it takes people with special skills to tune and play a violin, it takes individuals with special skills to deal with different types of conflict. Let's face it. Chances are you don't want an automobile mechanic tuning your violin. Different conflict ministry styles are needed in various conflict situations. Factors such as the congregation's size and age, issues, personalities involved, and intensity of the conflict can affect the style needed.

A spaceship breaking gravity to achieve orbit is tension and conflict that leads to a great outcome. Reentering earth's atmosphere is also an action of resistance and conflict that has been an even larger challenge to the NASA space program. Great risk is involved. However, a positive outcome is generally worth the risk. The alternative is to remain in space forever and avoid the reentry conflict.

Numerous congregations avoid their challenges, unwilling to address them for fear of harmful conflict. These congregations need a little conflict along their journey through which they can become conflict literate.

Often the best method for preventing unhealthy conflict is to educate congregations concerning the various types or intensities of conflict. Specifically, congregations need to learn how not to escalate conflict unnecessarily, but rather deal with issues of conflict when and where they occur. Those who are conflict illiterate need to become conflict literate.

At times congregations have antagonists present who promote unhealthy conflict. These antagonists may need to be confronted before they destroy the congregation. Congregations that have been hurt by antagonistic conflict need to be loved and taught a pattern of interpersonal relationship that will prevent them from returning to unhealthy patterns of conflict. As laborers for Christ, we all need to cultivate our talents and develop our skills in this area of congregational and denominational life. Unfortunately, local congregational tensions are currently increasing in many places.

Conflict is necessary. We could not live in a world without it. A church staff member in a congregation in which no conflict exists is probably in a congregation without strong Kingdom commitments. The book of Acts details how conflict was a necessary ingredient in the spread of the gospel.

Conflict is a necessary part of the Christian experience, as the old self comes in conflict with the new self. Daily we are in conflict to become more Christlike.

Therefore, we should not be afraid of healthy conflict. Rather, we should welcome it as an opportunity to bring forth positive spiritual and social change. We should meet unhealthy conflict as a challenge to the love of Christ, and the fellowship of the congregation.

The Christian who has made peace with God is not exempt from struggle and conflict, and history can testify that it is often the noblest saints who feel their unworthiness most.

The apostle Paul talks about personal conflict between his two natures in Romans 7:14–25. Verse 19 clearly expresses his dilemma. "For the good that I wish, I do not do; but I practice the very evil that I do not wish" As Christians we all face this struggle in our daily walk with the Lord.

Christians—such as Paul—who have made their peace with God are not exempt from struggle and conflict, and history can testify that often the noblest saints are the ones who feel their unworthiness most. As I write these words, yet another great international evangelical Christian leader has been forced to show his humanity—the conflict between these two natures. Intrapersonal conflict is a constant struggle for all of us.

The Acts of the Apostles is a book of the Bible full of empowering conflict situations. It begins with the initial spread of the gospel that was propelled forward by the dramatic coming of the Holy Spirit on the day of Pentecost.

The early church sought to huddle in Jerusalem. The persecution by those who did not embrace Jesus led to the Church being scattered. Chapters 8—11 of the Acts of the Apostles recount various incidents of people in internal conflict and people taking external action to spread the gospel beyond Jerusalem, beyond the core Jewish culture, and to the Gentiles. In chapter 11, at Antioch these followers of Jesus were first called Christians.

The Council at Jerusalem recorded in chapter 15 speaks loudly to an early conflict in the Church as to who could be a Christian and under what circumstances. The result empowered the gospel to spread throughout the world with the blessings of the founding apostles. The council's conflict was ultimately a healthy one, although it probably did not seem like it to those experiencing it.

Conflict Is about Power and Control

One of the central manifestations of sin in the twenty-first century is our neurotic need for control. For all the control we attempt, we can never seem to control what matters most—our relationship to God. The more we clamor to be in control or in charge, the more we squeeze life out of everything that is precious to us.

Control changes people, and even the best-intentioned are perverted by it. Control seeks to deny progress to others. Control is non-risking and avoids the call of God.

Power, at its best, has a creative nature to it. The apostles were told in the first chapter of Acts about the power they would receive when the Holy Spirit came upon them. God's power transforms people.

Let's visit a couple of simple, yet profound, theological views on power and control. God seeks to empower us. Satan seeks to control us. God seeks to help us to be all that we can be in the kingdom of God. Satan seeks to keep us from being what Satan does not want us to be.

God adds to. Satan takes away from. God pulls us forward. Satan drags us back. God calls us to unconditional love. Satan calls us to place so many conditions on our love that it is no longer love.

God urges us to positively act on the principles of the gospel. Satan urges us to negatively act on the positions represented by winning and self-reward.

Healthy conflict has hope as a characteristic. Unhealthy conflict has despair as a characteristic. Those with hope in eternal life aren't shaken by conflict.

Your theology profoundly shapes the way you approach conflict. If you believe there is hope for the next world, if you believe that death is not ultimate, if you believe that out of failure can come new life, new opportunity, new growth and hope, then conflict can be a positive motivating force.

The Seven Intensities of Conflict

Conflict can be healthy, transitional, or unhealthy. Getting a clear view on what dimension or intensity of conflict you may be experiencing in any given situation can be difficult. I am grateful to Speed Leas for his pioneering work in assessing conflict situations. More than twenty years ago he developed an understanding of the stages or levels of conflict.

His work is also very helpful in acting as a beginning point for figuring what positive, proactive actions to take at what stage or level of conflict. Over the past two decades I have modulated his work into seven intensities of conflict that mirror his five stages or levels. (See the chart at the end of this chapter.)

The first three intensities represent healthy typical conflict experienced in congregations and many other arenas of life. When I claim that every congregation needs a little conflict, I am referencing these first three intensities. The theme for addressing these healthy intensities is "Getting to *Yes!*" This means that the focus of efforts at these intensities are coming to an agreement or attaining a resolution to the presenting situation.

The fourth intensity is a transitional intensity between conflict that is healthy and conflict that is unhealthy. The theme for addressing this intensity is "Getting Past *No!*" This involves the desire to avoid a negative outcome and impact by focusing on signs of hope. The goal of leaders is to mediate the situation to achieve a reasonably positive outcome and impact.

Intensities five, six, and seven represent unhealthy dimensions of conflict, which the vast majority of congregations are ill-prepared to address. The theme for addressing these intensities of unhealthy conflict is "Getting to *Neutral!*" Damage to the congregation has occurred that cannot be ignored and will be difficult to repair. How do we get to a neutral place to create a new beginning?

These unhealthy intensities of conflict require conflict literacy, emotional maturity, and spiritual maturity not seen in the typical congregation. They also require outside, third-party assistance to address them.

The next seven chapters will each take one of these intensities of conflict and seek to further develop it. I urge you to read all seven chapters, and not just view the chart at the end of this chapter and focus only on the intensity you believe is currently present in your congregation. Do this for two reasons. First, you may be wrong about which intensity is currently present in your congregation and take incorrect actions that will not provide the most loving ministry possible at that intensity. Second, you need to learn why every congregation needs a little conflict, and you can best discover this by becoming conflict literate about intensities one through three.

COACHING INSIGHTS

■ Before reading this chapter, how did you view conflict? In what ways did you see it as unnecessary and unhealthy? In what ways did you see it as necessary and healthy?

■ What has been your typical response to conflict? Do you avoid it, accommodate more forceful people, attack those who are in conflict with you, dialogue with people regarding conflict, stay focused on the issues, or focus on the people?

■ What are some of your new learnings from this chapter that have changed your viewpoint? What positive actions that will be helpful to your congregation do you plan to take as a result of your new learnings?

■ What is your theology of conflict? Where is God in conflict? Where are you as a creation of God in conflict? Where are the people with whom you find yourself in conflict in your theology of conflict?

■ What are some of the applications to this way of looking at conflict to other parts of your life? What are some actions you need to commit to taking in those arenas?

PERSONAL REFLECTIONS

Your Reflections: What are your reflections on the material presented in this chapter?

_____

_____

_____

_____

_____

Your Actions: What actions do you need to take about your life, ministry, and/or congregation based on the material presented in this chapter?

_____

_____

_____

_____

_____

Your Accountability: How and by whom do you want to be held accountable for taking these actions?

_____

_____

_____

_____

_____

The Intensities of Congregational Conflict

INTENSITY ONE	INTENSITY TWO	INTENSITY THREE	INTENSITY FOUR	INTENSITY FIVE	INTENSITY SIX	INTENSITY SEVEN
Healthy	Healthy	Healthy	Transitional	Unhealthy	Unhealthy	Unhealthy
Getting to Yes!	Getting to Yes!	Getting to Yes!	Getting Past No!	Getting to Neutral!	Getting to Neutral!	Getting to Neutral!
Identifiable Task-Oriented Issues with Many Solutions	Relationship-Oriented Disagreements over Multiple Issues	Competition within a Group or between Groups	Congregational-Wide Competition with Voting	Congregational-Wide Combat with Organizational Casualties	Pursuit of People beyond the Congregation Focused on Their Integrity	Intentional Physical Harm to People or Congregational Facilities
Win-Win	Win-Win	Win-Lose	Win-Lose	Lose-Leave	Lose-Lose	Lose-Lose
Conflict Resolution	Conflict Resolution	Conflict Mediation	Conflict Mediation	Conflict Management	Conflict Management	Conflict Management
[Chaplain or Personal Coach]	[Chaplain or Personal Coach]	[Team Coach or Mediator]	[Organizational Coach, Mediator, or Consultant]	[Consultant or Arbitrator]	[Arbitrator or Attorney]	[Law Enforcement]
--------	--------	--------	*Compel*	*Compel*	*Compel*	*Compel*
--------	--------	*Negotiate*	*Negotiate*	*Negotiate*	*Negotiate*	*Negotiate*
Collaborate	*Collaborate*	*Collaborate*	*Collaborate*	--------	--------	--------
Persuade	*Persuade*	*Persuade*	--------	--------	--------	--------
Accommodate	*Accommodate*	--------	--------	--------	--------	--------
Avoid	*Avoid*	--------	--------	--------	*Avoid*	*Avoid*
Support	*Support*	*Support*	*Support*	*Support*	*Support*	*Support*

[Adapted by George Bullard of The Columbia Partnership, Columbia, SC, from five levels of conflict originated by Speed Leas of The Alban Institute, Herndon, VA.] January 24, 2008 Edition, Copyright 2007, Rev. George Bullard, D.Min., www.BullardJournal.org.

2

The First Intensity of Conflict

Typical Issues with Many Solutions

EXECUTIVE SUMMARY

The purpose of this chapter is to dialogue about the first intensity of conflict, which involves typical, normal, or expected issues encountered in congregations. The focus will be on the many right answers that exist at this juncture and on the great opportunity for helping congregational leaders and participants develop healthy patterns of decision-making that will allow them to engage low to medium intensity conflict without experiencing unnecessary harm from their conflict situations. This is a win-win intensity where everyone can come away feeling good about the addressing of identified issues.

Image of Intensity One

Intensity one conflict is like a single stream flowing from the mountains toward a valley. It is experienced as a task-oriented, clear stream with cool water that winds down from the mountains and along the way provides power for the paddle wheel of a former small gristmill that is now a museum. It flows by several serene, wooded picnic areas where families are often seen enjoying picnics and play together. It symbolizes the daily qualities and challenges of individuals, families, and congregational life.

Overview of Intensity One Conflict

Every congregation needs intensity one conflict situations. Intensity one conflict is a single, identifiable, task-oriented issue with many solutions. It is not person-oriented. Nothing is wrong with or disagreeable about people. Something is not as good or right as it could be about how the issue is addressed.

The issue can be something such as the heat and cooling in the worship center, choosing the curriculum to be taught in specific Sunday school classes or small groups, choosing the color of the new hymnal for the church, choosing the design for redecorating the fellowship hall, fixing the leaking roof in the preschool areas, determining the order of worship for a particular Sunday, or addressing a scheduling conflict between a church event and a community event being held in the church facilities.

The issue may involve confused or otherwise unclear communication. If so, this part of the issue can be cleared up quickly. An intensity one issue, however, goes beyond simple communication glitches and represents a real issue. People involved understand and appreciate one another, but they just have different perspectives on the issue. Some emotion or even anger may be expressed; but it is briefly expressed, and most, if not all, the people involved can move beyond it. If expressions of anger are sustained, this is a sign of a higher intensity of conflict, or possible dysfunction in a specific person.

People who cannot manage their own emotions and behavior at intensity one are signaling something deeper may be going on with them. They are connecting this specific issue, or the people involved, with a deeper level of dissatisfaction and anger.

The idea at intensity one is that the identified issue can be assessed, analyzed, and addressed. It is tangible. The various folks involved can agree on a definition that shows this to be the right issue. It can be a win-win situation. Resolution is probable if appropriate people genuinely engage it.

Multiple intensity one conflicts can be going on at the same time. If they are unrelated or isolated to different parts of the congregation, then there is no systemic problem or higher intensity conflict. If they are related and spread throughout the congregation, they are generally signs of a deeper intensity of conflict that people are avoiding.

Congregational Illustrations of Intensity One

Staff and Worship Conflict in Good Shepherd Church

An example of intensity one conflict is when the pastor and music director are working together to have a smooth-flowing and meaningful worship service. They must work regularly on fitting the critical elements of worship into a worshipful flow. There are many right ways to do this. The pastor comes from a liturgical worship tradition, and the music director from a praise and worship approach.

They must continually work on varying the elements of worship, connecting with the congregation in worship, and both feeling good about the quality of worship. They realize there are various good ways to do this, and they generally work hard to achieve excellent worship.

In addition, they have a worship team in the congregation who works with them to plan and carry out worship. The pastor and the music director are sensitive to the need for unity to exist between them to help this team be motivated to lead worship. Also, they are sensitive to involving this team in the ownership of high quality worship. To do this they seek to listen to and address the issues raised by the team.

They have worked with the worship team to study books and resources on worship so there is a common theology, philosophy, and style approach to worship. Even so, individual issues still arise from time to time that must be addressed appropriately.

Leadership vs. Management in Trinity Church

Intensity one conflict occurs when the heat and air conditioning at Trinity church is not working right in part of the building. This is a continual problem, but it does have several possible solutions. The people impacted by the problem know the people responsible for properties' issues are dealing with the issue and soon it will be resolved.

At first the trustees did not know about the severity of the heat and air conditioning situation. However, the groups that meet in that part of the building patiently talk with the trustees about this issue until the groups are satisfied the trustees understand and are working on it.

Everyone is aware the buildings are old and require a lot of continual maintenance. There is just not enough money to deal with all the issues at once, and recent efforts to raise additional money have gone well, but have still not covered the necessary expenses. No one is upset at this juncture, because everyone knows everything reasonable is being done to resolve building maintenance issues.

Women's Bible Study Group in Grace Church

Intensity one conflict is similar to a situation in a women's Bible study group in which Emily is the teacher, and Kim is one of her best friends and a student in the class. Their Bible study group is trying to decide what to study for the next season. The choices they are reviewing include (1) a thematic Bible study on various topics of relevance to spiritual formation stages in the life of a Christian disciple, and (2) a Bible book series that goes verse by verse and chapter by chapter through various books of the Bible.

Emily wants to teach the thematic Bible study, and Kim wants to study a Bible book series. They cannot decide what to do. They determine to ask their pastor, whom they respect very much. So they approach their pastor one Sunday and ask his opinion. A foolish pastor would tell them; a wise pastor would dialogue with them about the values of the various approaches, and turn them around and send them back into their study group to make their own decision. Why?

At intensity one conflict, several-to-many right answers exist for every situation. Unless the pastor is extremely controlling, or has a strong need to be needed, the pastor should not provide easy answers for intensity one conflict situations. Rather, the pastor should use them as opportunities to help these congregational participants practice healthy decision-making so they will raise their capacity to handle easy to moderately difficult decisions.

Addressing Intensity One Conflict

"Getting to *Yes!*" is the theme of intensity one conflict. Everyone should be able to enthusiastically affirm the process, the outcome, and the impact of dealing in a healthy manner with intensity one conflict.

The key point to remember is that intensity one conflict issues are win-win situations. Everyone can win, and everyone needs to take actions that empower themselves and everyone else to win. Demanding to win at intensity one escalates it to an intensity two or three. Accepting a loss at intensity one escalates it to an intensity two or three. Therefore, let a one be a one.

Keep issues specific and singular. Focus only on the issue at hand, and do not drag other issues into the dialogue. Identify the source of the issue, assess it, analyze it if you like, and activate a solution for the issue. Brainstorming possible solutions is a very helpful exercise at intensity one conflicts because it can lead to creative solutions everyone can address that might not have been solutions anyone had thought about before.

Providing a solution acceptable to everyone is the key. At intensity one, this is not difficult. It is not about fixing the people who are involved. All the way through addressing the issue, share full information using clear, specific language oriented to the present and not casting blame.

People who are directly impacted by an issue need to address it. Intensity one is a great time and place for people to learn good, healthy decision-making skills. Encourage participation by all persons involved. Work at the lowest level of authority and decision-making in the congregation. Do not appeal to higher authorities—especially the pastor, or, generally, even staff members. The pastor's involvement may actually be unnecessary and harmful to the long-term conflict ministry within the congregation.

Many good and loving solutions to issues exist at this intensity. Involve only the people who need to be involved in addressing this issue. When the solution is activated, celebrate the solution; and praise everyone who was involved in providing the solution. At that point involvement of the pastor in helping you celebrate a great win-win action might be appropriate.

Consensus Issue Statements

A technique to be learned at intensity one conflict is the development of *consensus issue statements*. These are statements developed by all parties involved that clearly state the issue in language that is as neutral as possible. The best statement is one that everyone affirms to be an accurate statement of the issue, and everyone believes that if the consensus issue statement can be effectively addressed, then the issue will be resolved.

Here are some examples of consensus issues statements.

- Regulating the temperature in the worship center is a challenge that goes beyond the personal temperature preferences of people in attendance. The spirit of worship can be enhanced by discovering a way to regulate the temperature for greater comfort among the attendees.
- Multiple viewpoints exist in our Sunday school class (or small group) concerning the curriculum that we should study for the next season. Various class (or small group) participants

are at different places in their spiritual development, and each wants a curriculum that speaks to his or her next stage of development.

• The typical time in the order of worship when babies are dedicated or christened will make it impossible for the grandfather of one of the babies to observe the event because of a work responsibility he has every Sunday morning. An earlier time during the worship service would make it possible for him to attend, but some are opposed to changing the order of worship.

When developing a consensus issue statement, this is a good time to identify the issue as one of attitudes, emotions, communication, or one that is substantive in nature. Too often issues are about attitudes, emotions, and communication. Too infrequently they are about true substantive issues. A substantive issue is a real, actual, objective, factual issue as opposed to a subjective issue or matter of opinion.

A consensus issue statement generally implies a way forward. Providing a way forward is an important principle to learn at intensity one conflict. In addition, the higher the intensity of conflict, the more helpful a consensus issue statement becomes.

COACHING BREAK

✔ Gaze out the window for a minute. Ponder the situation of your congregation. What images come to mind?

✔ What are examples of intensity one conflicts that regularly arise in the life and ministry of your congregation? How does your congregation handle these issues? How are you able to keep these conflicts focused on the issue and not on the people?

✔ When you think about your experience with intensity one issues, in those situations were you able to focus on "Getting to *Yes!*" or did you feel the need to win? How would you address some of these issues differently knowing that intensity one is a win-win situation?

✔ How can you apply the principle of finding a way forward by beginning with a consensus issue statement? Experiment with trying to write a consensus issue statement for some of the issues your congregation faces.

What Can Go Right at Intensity One?

1. Issues can be clearly defined.
2. Solutions can be quickly achieved.
3. Everyone can learn how to deal with intensity one conflicts.
4. Emotional currency can be developed that will empower the congregation to deal with tougher issues.
5. Laypersons can step forward as people who are learning how to deal with conflict rather than counting on the pastor and staff to deal with every conflict.
6. People who are emotionally out of step can be identified, and the life issues they are facing can be addressed.
7. Issues can actually be resolved to the point they may not occur again.

What Can Go Wrong at Intensity One?

1. Participants can fail to engage deeply and not clearly define the issue or issues.
2. People involved can allow the issue or issues to drag out and thus initiate a process of escalation as people become angry with people rather than issues.
3. Engagement happens haphazardly, and people really do not learn from the experience.
4. Emotional currency is developed in only a few people because some do not see the connection between how low intensity conflicts are handled and how higher intensity conflicts are handled.
5. To resolve the issue the pastor or a staff person becomes involved when their involvement is really unnecessary, and thus moves the situation from one of consensus building to one of being persuaded by an authority figure as to the outcome.
6. Individuals who act badly in the conflict are not clearly identified, and their life issues are not addressed.
7. The issue or issues may appear to be resolved until one day they come up again in an unexpected manner.

Every Congregation Needs Intensity One
Conflict Situations

Intensity one conflict situations are empowering to congregations. They represent great opportunities for learning. At intensity one, skills can be developed in making healthy decisions.

Decision-making principles can be stated and practiced at a time when position and personality are not issues. Decision makers learn there are many right answers at intensity one.

Participants in a conflict can learn to make decisions at the lowest possible level of authority in the congregation, involving only the necessary people. Learning this skill helps keep conflict from being something that is unnecessarily escalated at other intensities. At intensity one, participants in the conflict can hear the principle-based passion of others without unhealthy emotion being expressed.

The key learning is that every congregation needs intensity one conflict situations.

A Congregation Who Handled Intensity One Conflict Well

Southside was not formed out of ideal circumstances. It was a separation group from another congregation. Over several weeks other families joined, wanting to be part of this new congregation because of its theology, missional approach, and worship style.

Very early in the life of the congregation diverse points of view were expressed about many issues. The congregants were highly motivated to build a new healthy culture, but had no heritage together or formal procedures. Many issues were brought to the attention of the pastor, who was asked to make a ruling or decision.

Quickly the pastor became aware that a healthy process for fixing even task-oriented issues was needed. Without full knowledge of the concept of consensus issue statements, the pastor worked with an informal group of wise leaders to suggest a healthy process. It involved dialogue among only the impacted people, development of a concise consensus issue statement, agreement on a way forward, informal accountability for full resolution, and—in the spirit of the biblical creation story—a way to declare completion of dialogue and the goodness of the results.

Early in the life of Southside this became hardwired into their culture and helped them develop other processes for more intense conflict.

COACHING INSIGHTS

■   Before reading this chapter, how did you handle intensity one conflict? Could you correctly diagnose it, or did you always think that any conflict was bad and more intense than has been described here?

■ What has gone right in the way you have handled intensity one conflicts in your congregation? What has gone wrong? What would you do differently?

■ If you are the pastor, a staff minister, or a program staff member, to what extent have you involved yourself in intensity one conflicts? What are some examples in which you have empowered others to deal with their own conflicts rather than getting involved yourself?

■ How would you define solution or resolution of conflict at intensity one? When is it over? When is it likely to come up again? How can you tell the difference, and what might you do at the time of the conflict to address this?

■ Are there intensity one conflicts you ought to simply avoid, or in which you should accommodate the viewpoint of someone else? Or do you feel the need to address every intensity one conflict? If so, when do you have time to do anything else except address conflict?

■ What reasons do you believe support the premise that every congregation needs intensity one conflict situations? What can be learned from these situations that may empower the future life and ministry of your congregation? How can you share these learnings throughout your congregation and thus increase your capacity to handle conflict situations?

PERSONAL REFLECTIONS

Your Reflections: What are your reflections on the material presented in this chapter?

Your Actions: What actions do you need to take about your life, ministry, and/or congregation based on the material presented in this chapter?

_____

_____

_____

_____

_____

Your Accountability: How and by whom do you want to be held accountable for taking these actions?

_____

_____

_____

_____

_____

3

The Second Intensity of Conflict

Common Disagreements over Multiple Issues

EXECUTIVE SUMMARY

The purpose of this chapter is to dialogue about the second intensity of conflict, which involves common, ordinary, and anticipated disagreements between people in a congregation over multiple issues. The focus will be on handling the regular emotional issues that arise between people who are not sufficiently in spiritual community with one another and have not developed the emotional maturity to handle common disagreements. Handling their disagreement at this intensity can be a very healthy process for personal growth among leaders and participants in congregations. This is a win-win intensity in which almost everyone can work through the interpersonal relationship issues.

Image of Intensity Two Conflict

Intensity two conflict is like three streams flowing from the mountains toward a valley. The first stream (being borrowed from the intensity one example) is a task-oriented stream. The second stream is a relationship-oriented stream. It, too, is crystal clear, fed by a spring and has unspoiled water ready for bottling. The third stream is perceived to be a hidden agenda stream. It is muddy, high in iron content, full of other minerals, not pleasing as drinking water, and considered hard water requiring water softener for even household use. Such a stream is also an experience of congregational life.

Overview of Intensity Two Conflict

Every congregation needs intensity two conflict situations.

Intensity two conflict is a disagreement between people, rather than a challenge concerning an issue. Personalities are now involved. At intensity two some emotion is typically expressed because people, generally individuals, are not getting along well with one another.

In any given situation, rather than there being just one active issue, there are at least three active issues: (1) a task-oriented issue concerning an attitude, an emotion, communication, or substantive information on a particular issue; (2) a relationship issue that means some days the people involved really do not get along though supposedly they are friends; (3) and a hidden issue—generally an emotional issue of something one person has against another person—hidden because the person is not talking about it, and the other person may not even *know that* it exists, much less *what* it is.

A new element of shrewdness and calculation emerges at intensity two conflict. Planning strategies for the next encounter with the problem person or persons is a goal of participants. The issue or issues have shifted from the need to address the issue or problem, to the need to address the problem person or persons.

At times you must hold pre-meetings to plan a strategy for dealing with problem persons and/or post-meetings to determine how to spin the information or a report that is likely to come out of the meeting. Giving assignments for people to quietly handle various relationships and aspects would be typical.

Self-protection is an objective of people involved in intensity two conflicts. Everyone involved wants to resolve the issue or fix the problem. In doing so, they want to come away looking good and having everyone like them.

In some cases, language shifts from specific to general. In consulting with a congregation recently, I always knew the laity were talking about the pastor when they said, "We have a leadership issue." At times people stop naming individuals with whom they are having difficulty and refer to people using general language. Feelings and relationships are cautious, tense, but not hostile. Some information considered harmful is withheld because sharing it will make the person who shares it look bad.

Humor can have a hostile edge in such situations. Something is said in a joking manner, but it is more than a joke. Also, some common phrases used at intensity two conflicts are: "We don't communicate well here." "We don't trust each other enough." "I am disappointed in that person."

In intensity two conflict, the issues of intensity one conflict are restated to include the appearance of blaming. For example, someone wonders if the new custodian knows how to work the thermostat, or if the trustees are telling him where to set the thermostat so they can save money while the congregation freezes or cooks.

In another instance, a person wonders if someone, perhaps the Christian education or small groups leader, is attempting to manipulate each Sunday school class (or small group) to teach certain literature rather than giving them the freedom to choose what they have enjoyed for several years.

Congregational Illustrations of Intensity Two
Staff and Worship Conflict in Good Shepherd Church

Intensity two conflict occurs when the pastor and music director seek to move deeper into the transition of worship and begin to disagree over worship content, style, length, and other elements. The pastor, who desires to begin preaching about thirty minutes into the service, is regularly not beginning the sermon until forty minutes into the worship service. The music director keeps adding elements to worship at the last minute that were not part of worship planning, and improvising in the middle of worship.

Periodically on Monday mornings the pastor and music director have tense staff meetings in which they debate rather than dialogue about worship from the day before. Beyond this, unknown to the pastor, but known to a few people in the congregation, the music director and his wife are having some marital problems. She did not marry a congregational minister, but a secular musician. Now she is struggling with the role expectations on her as a minister's wife. She wants to enjoy a social life she feels is restricted by her husband's role in congregational life.

Leadership vs. Management in Trinity Church

Intensity two conflict develops when the new heating system is put in place, but unresolved issues emerge. Some of these are people issues. The part of the building served by the new heating and air conditioning system has both men and women's groups, and both young adults and senior adults meeting in it. Somehow each group thought that when the new system was put in place individual thermostats would be in each room, but that is not what occurred.

Trinity's finance committee wanted to cut the cost and so blocked the trustees from spending the extra money it would cost to purchase a system that allows for individually regulated thermostats. The finance committee refused to allocate sufficient funds for things they thought were not needed. Now each Sunday involves competition between the various classes over the temperature at which the thermostat is set.

Hearing these complaints, the church custodian says he can fix the problem for a small amount of money, as he knows about HVAC and electrical wiring. The trustees scrape up the money and authorize the custodian to do the work without asking him exactly what he is going to do. What he does is install dummy thermostats in each room that can be turned on and off, and the temperature supposedly adjusted, but nothing really happens. For a while everyone seems to be satisfied because they think they are able to control the temperature. Thus a hidden agenda has been established because only the custodian, who is also a member of Trinity, knows the truth.

Women's Bible Study Group in Grace Church

Intensity two conflict arises when the women's Bible study group has planned a fellowship gathering to spend some quality time together and to decide what curriculum they will use for the next season. Emily and Kim have continued to focus on their respective preferred curriculum choices of the thematic discipleship study and the Bible book study.

Prior to the gathering, Emily calls several friends in the group, other than Kim, to solicit their support for the thematic discipleship study. She is careful to tell them that Kim has a different perspective and that while Emily really wants to teach the discipleship study, she does not want to offend her friend Kim.

Kim also makes some telephone calls. Her calls are of a similar style and content as Emily's. She does add one factor. She reminds people that Emily only has a high school education, whereas Kim has a master's degree in teaching. The curriculum Emily wants to teach is a particularly difficult curriculum and probably needs a teacher with more education. This supports Kim's assertion that the Bible book study, a much simpler study, would better fit the skill of Emily.

The decision around what curriculum to study had now become a disagreement between friends. Plus, one more element has arisen at intensity two conflict: the hidden agenda. Emily has a sixteen-year-old son, and Kim has a fifteen-year-old daughter. A couple of weeks ago at an all-day congregational youth group outing, Emily's son and Kim's daughter got separated from the rest of the youth group for over an hour. Each mother is suspicious that the other mother's child led her child into some undefined, inappropriate behavior during that time. Neither teenager is talking, but each is denying that anything went on. Emily and Kim have not talked with each other about this.

Addressing Intensity Two Conflict

"Getting to *Yes!*" is the theme of intensity two conflict, as it was in intensity one. The process may be a little rocky at first because of the interpersonal relationships and the hidden agenda. If, however, the primary participants in the conflict are willing to engage it in a healthy manner, it can be resolved.

The key point to remember is that intensity two conflict disagreements are still win-win situations. Although they may not act like it at first, everyone really wants everyone to win. A win-lose outcome is not the long-term impact anyone desires. However, it can be the outcome if the disagreements between individual people are not handled in positive, proactive ways.

In intensity two conflicts, you should keep issues separated from one another. Do not let them merge into a larger, combined issue that will be more difficult to handle. Develop a distinct consensus issue statement for each separate issue, giving priority to the ones participants consider easiest to identify, assess, analyze, and address. As you dialogue on each statement, allow people to identify them as one with which they are concerned.

At times, people will not readily come forward to admit a particular issue is one with which they are concerned. Therefore, if you suspect someone is holding back their feelings and involvement in a particular issue, gently question that person about the possibility he or she needs to accept some ownership of that issue.

Address issues one at a time, again beginning with the easiest ones to resolve. Gaining experience and establishing a pattern will allow the participants to bring their new experience in working together to the figurative "table" to dialogue about the more difficult issues.

One amazing thing will happen when you face multiple intensity two issues. As you address some of the easier ones, some of the other issues will begin to lessen in their intensity, and even disappear by the time you get to them. When several smaller issues are resolved that were part of a larger issue, the larger issue diminishes in its intensity and impact, and can be resolved.

To review, strategies for dealing with conflict at this intensity include the encouragement of participation. Participants should clearly identify issues in the form of consensus issue statements. Work at the lowest possible level within the congregation, involving as few people as possible, yet everyone who is necessary. Focus upon issues that unite the congregation and around which as many participants as possible have deep passion.

Encourage the expression of feelings in the presence of others with whom you do not agree. Encourage genuine statements of appreciation for one another. Encourage verbal prayers for one another. Encourage expression of the signs of health and strength in the relationships between the participants in the conflict.

Ground Rules

At intensity two conflict, intentional dialogue about ground rules for fair conflict engagement is necessary. Now that interpersonal relationships are involved, you must be sure people treat one another with respect as equals, see each other as persons of worth created in the image of God to live and to love, act in a trustworthy manner with one another, and handle information with appropriate confidentiality and privacy.

For these things to happen, at least one brief conversation should take place that establishes appropriate ground rules around how participants relate to one another. This is another great opportunity to build the capacity for handling greater intensities of conflict that may occur from time to time.

By intensity two conflicts it is already possible to discover that blind copies of e-mails, photocopies of written communication and documents, and other communication have been shared with a larger group of people than those primarily involved in the conflict dialogue. Appropriate ground rules should cover this type of communication as a part of confidentiality and privacy.

COACHING BREAK

✔ Gaze out the window for a minute. Ponder the situation of your congregation. What images come to mind?

✔ What are examples of intensity two conflicts that regularly arise in the life and ministry of your congregation? How does your congregation handle these issues? How are you able to keep these conflicts focused on the issues and the people who are primary participants, and not let them spread to other issues and people?

✔ When you think back about your previous experience with intensity two issues, on those occasions were you able to focus on "Getting to *Yes!*," or did you feel the need to win, particularly over a person you did not respect? How would you address some of these issues differently knowing that intensity two is still a win-win situation?

✔ What type of ground rules do you think need to govern an intensity two conflict situation? What ground rules would be most helpful and empowering of a position solution? What ground rules would actually be harmful and controlling?

What Can Go Right at Intensity Two?

1. Meaningful engagement of both the relevant issues and the meaningful relationships between people can occur.
2. Reasonable and true solutions can often be achieved if participants are willing to deeply engage the process of great decision-making coupled with focused relationship-building.
3. Everyone can learn how to deal with intensity two conflict situations.
4. Deeper, more meaningful relationship, even among people who are already friends, can emerge and be helpful to deepening the sense of fellowship and community in the congregation.
5. Once the emotion expressed in disagreements becomes part of the conflict process, the opportunity is significant for laypersons and church staff to learn how to deal with the more complicated conflict of intensity two.
6. People who are emotionally unprepared to deal with complex and ambiguous situations can be discovered, and the spiritual

and emotion growth issues of their life and ministry can be addressed.

7. Complex issues between individuals can actually be resolved in a manner such that they may not resurface in future years.

What Can Go Wrong at Intensity Two?

1. Participants can fail to engage with their full heart, soul, mind, and strength. They can hold something back. Those involved in the conflict dialogue may never know about the hidden agenda of one or more of the participants.
2. Without full, clear, and genuine communication, reasonable and true solutions may not occur.
3. Since participants may fail to fully engage, then the hoped-for learnings from the experience may not occur, and the potential benefit for later intensity two conflicts or ones of greater intensity may not exist.
4. The opportunity may be lost for deeper, more meaningful relationships that can result from people being involved in mild conflict situations with one another.
5. The dialogue may not achieve resolution, and participants walk away realizing they are going to face these same people in a similar situation again.
6. Some participants engage in bad behavior during the dialogue around issues and relationships, creating an ongoing divide in the relationships.
7. The empowerment that could have been possible if resolution had been achieved is lost for now, and perhaps forever.

Every Congregation Needs Intensity Two Conflict Situations

Intensity two conflict situations are empowering to congregations. They represent additional great opportunities for learning. At intensity two, skills can be developed in dealing with the attitudes, emotions, and communication challenges that are part of conflict situations. These are added to the substantive issues from conflict intensity one.

Congregations need to learn how to develop community when participants in the congregation express a diversity of cultural perspectives. With the addition at intensity two of position and personality, congregations can learn essential skills in how to form community among people with a diversity of views on various subjects. Many right answers still exist because numerous, legitimate viewpoints are expressed by the people involved.

The key learning is that every congregation needs intensity two conflict situations.

A Congregation Who Handled Intensity Two Conflict Well

Greg Holland came to Temple following the pastorate of Samuel Wright. Samuel came to Temple straight out of seminary and stayed thirty-seven years. His knowledge of the church family and his emotional ties with people were deep. He and his wife remained active members of Temple following retirement, although he was away preaching many Sundays.

Often when people died, Samuel was the first person called. Many times Samuel was lined up to do the funeral before Greg even knew the person had died. On too many occasions when Greg went to visit someone in the hospital, Samuel had already visited them. In congregational business sessions people would quote what Samuel had said to them about issues currently under consideration.

Greg became increasingly angry at this behavior, but felt powerless to deal with it because of the influence Samuel still had in the congregation. He knew he had to find a way to confront Samuel. He was seeking to figure out how to approach it when Samuel stopped by the church one day to talk.

To his credit, Samuel recognized the problem and knew he and Greg had to work it out. On Samuel's part, he did not feel Greg was responding appropriately to the pastoral needs of these people Samuel had loved for so many years. As would logically happen, the people who were becoming some of Greg's best friends in the congregation were some of Samuel's detractors.

Greg and Samuel were both able to talk through various issues during several conversations. A great outcome was a set of ground rules they agreed to as to how they would relate to one another going forward. One action each engaged in was to go to people in the congregation and community where one had spoken negatively of the other and share the new depth of positive relationship they were building.

Coaching Insights

Before reading this chapter, how did you handle intensity two conflicts? Could you correctly diagnose them, or did you become confused with multiple issues coming your way that included the complexity of emotion and hidden agendas?

What has gone right in the way you have handled intensity two conflicts in your congregation? What has gone wrong? What would you do differently?

If you are the pastor, a staff minister, or a program staff member, what have you learned about leading and managing conflict as you have addressed intensity two conflict situations? What are examples of how you have appropriately involved others in dealing with intensity two conflict situations?

How would you define solution or resolution of conflict at intensity two? When is it over? When is it likely to come up again? How can you tell the difference, and what might you do at the time to address this?

Are there intensity two conflicts you ought to simply avoid, or in which you should accommodate the viewpoint of someone else? Or, do you feel the need to address every intensity two conflict? If so, when do you have time to do anything else except address conflict?

What reasons do you believe support the premise that every congregation needs intensity two conflict situations? What can be learned from these situations that may empower the future life and ministry of your congregation? How can you share these learnings throughout your congregation and thus increase your capacity to handle conflict situations?

PERSONAL REFLECTIONS

Your Reflections: What are your reflections on the material presented in this chapter?

_____

_____

_____

_____

_____

Your Actions: What actions do you need to take about your life, ministry, and/or congregation based on the material presented in this chapter?

_____

_____

_____

_____

Your Accountability: How and by whom do you want to be held accountable for taking these actions?

_____

_____

_____

_____

_____

4

The Third Intensity of Conflict

Competition That Develops Causes

EXECUTIVE SUMMARY

The purpose of this chapter is to dialogue about the third intensity of conflict, in which the conflict between people becomes competition within or between groups in the congregation. The focus will be on helping groups in congregations develop healthy patterns of decision-making when there is a genuine difference of perspective, multiple visions, and a diversity of passions about the past, present, and future of the congregation and about the correct way to address the next steps in the life of the congregation. For the first time a win-lose perspective is present as a felt need begins to arise to win because of the rightness or goodness of a particular cause.

Image of Intensity Three Conflict

Intensity three conflict is like five or more streams flowing from the mountains, hills, and out of natural springs that come together near the valley to form a river of concern. The river is powerful and provides many resources for the valley.

If you stand on the bank of the river and stick your hand in, how can you tell from which one of the five or more streams the water that your hand is touching is coming? You cannot. That is an image of what happens during intensity three conflict. The streams of issues that once were easy to identify are now impossible to distinguish. Issues of various kinds flow toward the valley, forming conflict concerns and causes in the life of the congregation.

Overview of Intensity Three Conflict

Every congregation needs intensity three conflict situations. Intensity three conflict involves a shift to a win-lose situation. For the first time people want to win. They realize that winning means other persons have to lose. They are not necessarily happy that their fellow congregational participants have to lose. But, they realize that for them to win, someone has to lose. And winning has now become important to them.

Often intensity three conflict situations occur when intensities one and two conflict situations are inappropriately handled and so escalate. The background of intensities one and two with the time already committed to this emerging and escalating conflict significantly diminishes trust between the participants in the conflict. Participants can fully resolve their conflict three situation only by restoring trust.

Competition within a group, or between groups, in the congregation is often at the core of intensity three conflict situations. This is not conflict throughout the congregation, but only in part of the congregation. Conflict that is congregation-wide would constitute intensity four conflict.

Intensity three conflict can be conflict within a class, a committee, the staff, or a program ministry or activity of the congregation. It can also be a conflict between groups in the congregation such as between the staff and the board, the finance committee and a specific ministry of the church, or between two Sunday school classes or two small groups.

Smaller membership congregations, with fewer than eighty people in average weekly worship attendance, face one unique challenge. They experience a fine line between parts of the congregation and the entire active congregation. As a result, intensity three conflict situations can quickly escalate to intensity four as news and gossip of the win-lose situation quickly spreads.

A very important principle for intensity three and greater conflict situations is that issues become meshed into causes. It is difficult, if not improbable to impossible, to distinguish the specific individual issues. This is symbolized many times by a definite shift in the language used at intensity three or greater conflict situations.

The tendency is for language to magnify and blow the conflict out of proportion. Examples of statements used are: "You always…," "She never…," "Everybody I know…," "Right-thinking people…," "Bible-believing people…," "Good Christians…"

With language and several other behaviors that emerge at intensity three conflict situations, a pattern of escalation begins. What are tendencies at intensity three conflict situations are urgencies at intensity four, and mandates at intensity five.

One behavior is the tendency to divide everything—every issue, every person, every relationship, and every cause—into polarities. Examples are: that which is right vs. that which is wrong, that which is good vs. that which is bad, that which is loving vs. that which is unloving, and that which is Christian versus that which is unchristian.

In intensity three conflict situations the tendency is to choose sides or causes that identify and distinguish the side's position on the issues at hand. This tendency becomes urgency at intensity four, at which point people are urged to choose sides. It becomes a mandate at intensity five. If you have not identified the side you are on by intensity five, then someone will claim you are on the other side. Neither side at intensity five conflict is willing to claim you or respect you if you do not choose loyalty to them.

This includes the pastor, staff ministers, and program staff leaders. Those pastors and staff who have avoided taking sides at intensities one and two are kindly asked at intensity three to reveal their preference. They are urged to do so at intensity four, and they are rejected at intensity five if they have not chosen the right side. This is why it is so difficult for pastors and staff ministers to lead and manage conflict when it goes beyond intensity three. They are no longer seen as neutral and may be rejected because some laypersons feel they have failed to show leadership by not taking a side.

Also at intensity three and greater, selected people seem to acquire a higher level of intelligence. Yeah, right! They exhibit this by appearing to be able to read the minds and motives of others. They say things such as, "Do you know why they did that? I'll tell you why they did that!" These people become students of the motives and actions of others. Such people contribute to a lack of reality and truth that begins to be experienced at intensity three conflict, and increases at subsequent intensities.

The manner in which prayer takes place is an important clue to intensity three conflict situations. When persons pray about the conflict situation at intensity three, they are generally praying with an open petition to God. A common phrase might be, "Holy God, what is your will in this situation?"

Examples of the types of concerns or causes that might be an occasion for intensity three conflict situations include, but are not limited to the following:

1. Starting a new worship service with a new style not favored by everyone.
2. Changing the criteria for who can serve as a deacon, elder, or board member in the congregation.
3. The calling of a new pastor or staff minister to the church, or actively accepting from the bishop the appointment of a new pastor or elder.
4. Discussing what new building to construct to deal with space issues, or how to carry out major renovation of existing buildings.
5. Dealing with difficulties in a major program of the congregation, such as the children or youth ministry.
6. Making major changes in staff employment policies.
7. Choosing the financial priorities for a capital stewardship campaign.
8. Engaging in a strategic planning process and seeking to determine the top priorities for the next three-to-five years.
9. Making changes in the financial support of the denominational programs.
10. Changing the schedule of Sunday morning activities, which will require people to choose a new worship service or a different Sunday school class or small group.
11. Deciding whether the weekday sports and recreation program is a ministry of the church or simply activities using the building. If they are simply using the building, then the congregation wants to charge them rent and utilities.
12. Determining whether the weekday preschool ought to pay rent to the church or be treated as a ministry of the church and not pay rent, even though it has a larger reserve fund than the church.

Some of these examples may appear to represent unhealthy intensities of conflict. In reality they are typical issues congregations regularly face. It is how congregations deal with them that determines whether they are played out as healthy and typical, or unhealthy and dysfunctional. Which way they are carried out is a conscious decision made by the leaders of the congregation.

Congregational Illustrations of Intensity Three

Staff and Worship Conflict in Good Shepherd Church

Intensity three conflict occurs when the worship choir and the worship committee get involved in the discussion about worship content, style, and length. The music director leads the worship choir, and the pastor relates to the worship committee. Part of the discussion becomes whether worship ought to be done the way the music director wants it or the way the pastor wants it.

In the eyes of the worship choir, the music director is the real leader of worship, has significantly and positively transformed worship over the past twelve-to-eighteen months, and the pastor's only role is to preach. In the eyes of the worship committee, the pastor is leading an annual plan of worship that loosely follows the liturgical calendar. The pastor is also aware of the events in the congregational life around which worship of God needs to be focused. The pastor has a clear preaching plan put together on an annual basis; the sermons are taped, reproduced, and distributed; and thus the preaching ought to be the focus of worship rather than the music.

Leadership vs. Management in Trinity Church

Intensity three conflict arises when the truth about the HVAC thermostats becomes known. This opens up a hostile dialogue between the groups that meet in that part of the building and the properties committee. Ultimately, the deeper truth is revealed: each classroom did not have a working thermostat because the finance committee would not approve the money for a system that allowed for working thermostats in each room. The solution is not as simple as just installing working thermostats, but rather a whole different type of HVAC system would need to be purchased.

Quickly, the frustration of the groups in that portion of the building shifts to discussion on how the congregation makes decisions and on the people who have perpetually controlled decisions in the life of the congregation. Many of the people seen as the blockers are on the finance committee, and they seem to always be on this committee. They may rotate off for a year, but then they are right back on the committee. The finance committee seeks to function as a self-appointed executive committee of the congregation. Angry people decide to try influencing the leadership nominating committee to get new and different people on the finance committee.

At the same time, the pastor has been leading the congregation in a spiritual strategic journey process to help the congregation journey in the direction of its full Kingdom potential. Using a strategic leadership coach provided by the denomination, the congregation has been writing a narrative story of its future ministry. Several new high-priority initiatives have been identified for which there is broad-based support throughout the congregation.

Recently, the pastor and several lay representatives of the vision fulfillment leadership community presented what they thought was a routine request to the finance committee for start-up funds for some of the new initiatives. The finance committee turned down the request—not because the money was not available, but because they did not agree with the priorities. Discussion ensued as to whether or not it was the role of the finance committee to veto priorities already embraced by the congregation. The finance committee indicated they did not care and were not going to allocate funds for the priorities.

Actions of the finance committee on both the HVAC system and on the vision fulfillment priorities become a point of discussion at the next meeting of the congregational board. Attempts are made to mediate these conflicts and clarify the role and authority of the finance committee. Mediation attempts extend over three months. It appears that a widening circle of people are becoming aware of the conflict between the controlling people on the finance committee and several other groups within the congregation. The board officers work hard to contain this controversy within the board, but it is a losing battle.

Women's Bible Study Group in Grace Church

Intensity three conflict develops when the gathering of the women's Bible study group, in which they were trying to decide what curriculum they would study, does not go well. Rather than focusing on which curriculum to teach, or whether to affirm the preference of Emily or Kim, the dialogue turns to the theology implied by the two curriculum choices.

Several people in the study group had taken a careful look at sample copies of the two curriculums. A couple of supporters of Kim indicate the thematic discipleship curriculum has some liberal theology in it that does not appear to be biblically based. They are not sure it is appropriate to study something that does not have a sound biblical base in a group whose focus is Bible study. Kim does not know this point of view is going to be brought up by one of her friends, but she supports this position once she hears it.

At the same time, Emily's next-door neighbor, who is member of another congregation in the community, raises concern about the narrow biblical view presented in the Bible book study curriculum and the insistence on a certain version of the Bible as being the only truly inspired version. In her church they use a gender-neutral version of the Bible, and she feels the curriculum is taking a fundamentalist approach.

Emily is uncertain what to do as she does not want to offend her study group, her friend Kim, nor her neighbor. Reluctantly she indicates she could supplement the curriculum with some other Bible study books if the group chose the Bible book series. The fellowship gathering ends without a decision being made. Several women in attendance report what happened in the meeting to the congregation's director of Christian education and other congregational leaders.

Addressing Intensity Three Conflict

"Getting to *Yes!*" is the theme of intensity three conflict, as it was in intensities one and two. Accomplishing this is more difficult and takes more intentional action than it did at lower intensities of conflict. Present at intensity three are substantive issues, impacted by attitudes, emotions, and communication barriers, clouded by the generalization of the issues into causes, and complicated by the desire of participants to win.

This sounds challenging, and is challenging. However, it is still a healthy intensity of conflict and often can be handled within the portion of the congregation experiencing the conflict. This will be true particularly if the participants have benefited from the learning provided during previous intensity one and two conflict situations.

At intensity three, encourage participation by all persons directly involved in the conflict, attempt collaborative problem-solving, utilize ground rules and trust development techniques, and help each participant see how they have contributed to the conflict.

Seek to identify consensus issues statements from within the various causes that have coalesced around the various issues. Identify these statements as intensity two or one issues, and deal with them at that intensity. Doing so has the potential to de-escalate the conflict to the point that an intensity three conflict situation is no longer present.

At times, third-party assistance is needed with intensity three conflict situations. Such assistance may be provided by a coach trained and experienced in working with groups or teams. At times, the assistance should be provided by a trained mediator. Beyond mediating the conflict, and perhaps de-escalating it so it can be resolved, the goal of this third-party assistance is to keep the conflict situation from escalating to an intensity four situation that spreads to the entire active congregation.

Often previous intensity three conflicts in congregations have left some unresolved issues. Some of these can be a decade or more old. When a new, similar concern or cause arises in a congregation, these old, unresolved issues once again come to the surface.

Old stories that involve both celebrations and fears are recounted during a new intensity three conflict concerning previous conflicts over similar issues. One example is dialogue around the issue of relocating the congregation to different facilities in another place. When such dialogue came up earlier, it was halted as an unacceptable issue for the congregation. Once it comes up again, people have stories of the previous time, unresolved feelings about their inability to work through the issues earlier, and perceived truthful information they bring to the dialogue that may or may not fit the current reality.

This is often a frustration for pastors, staff ministers, members, and regular attendees who were not present in the congregation when this issue was discussed and debated previously. For pastors this can be specifically frustrating if a former pastor took a stand on the issue, leading laypersons to assume the current pastor will take the same position. Before the pastor realizes what is going on, anger from the previous discussion is focused in his or her direction.

Trust Development

Trust between participants who find themselves in an intensity three conflict situation has been damaged. For full resolution to occur, trust must be restored. When trust is damaged, participants have lost confidence in the words, emotions, attitudes, and overall character of the people with whom they are in conflict. They question the integrity of people who may actually be among their best friends.

The longer trust is diminished, the more difficult it will be to restore trust. At the same time, participants in an intensity three conflict situation are highly motivated to restore trust with their friends or colleagues, but ego and lack of skill by one or more participating groups in dealing with conflict hinders this.

Trust development requires a deep commitment to love and respect the other, to believe the truthfulness of the other, and a willingness to address the relationship based on principles rather than positions. Trust is not something you demand from another person. It is something to extend to another person.

Often a third party needs to facilitate conversations between persons who have lost trust with one another. Clear, careful, compassionate conversation will be one key to restoring trust. Authentic, loving prayer for the other is an additional key to trust development. Unconditional love is a strong commitment to extend to the other during trust development, and regardless of the outcome of trust development conversations.

Personal Responses to Intensity Three Conflict

Various people respond to intensity three conflict situations differently. Some people feel personally attacked at intensity three and may overreact. Their overreaction escalates the conflict to intensity four, and perhaps intensity five conflict situations.

Pastors and other congregational staff ministers are particularly vulnerable to overreacting during intensity three conflict situations. They too quickly take intensity three as a threat to their leadership. They become concerned that a loss for them may threaten their tenure in their current ministry setting. Beyond that, losing their ministry position may threaten their ministry standing and the possibility of other desirable ministry placements or roles.

As a result, pastors and other congregational staff ministers may overreact. When they do so, they begin to focus the issues on themselves, and they eventually are perceived as the main or core problem, when they were not the cause or the origination of the conflict at all.

COACHING BREAK

✔ Gaze out the window for a minute. Ponder the situation of your congregation. What images come to mind?

✔ What examples of intensity three conflicts regularly arise in the life and ministry of your congregation? How does your congregation handle these issues? How are you able to keep these conflicts focused on the issues and the groups within the congregation who are primary participants without their spreading to other issues and groups?

✔ When you think back on your previous experience with intensity three issues, were you able to focus on "Getting to Yes!," or did you feel the need to win, particularly over persons or groups you did not respect? How would you address some of these issues differently knowing that intensity three is a win-lose situation, and you might lose?

✔ What type of trust development do you need to engage in during an intensity three conflict situation? What trust development steps would be most meaningful? How can you initiate restoration of relationships by extending trust to other participants?

What Can Go Right at Intensity Three?

1. Meaningful engagement can occur within groups or teams, or between groups or teams.
2. Reasonable and true solutions resulting from proactive collaboration can often be achieved.
3. Everyone can learn how to deal with intensity three conflict situations.
4. A greater commitment to the values, vision, and goals of the congregation can result from innovative and successful engagement of intensity three conflict situations.
5. Once the causes put forth in the competition are identified and addressed, the opportunity is significant for laypersons and church staff to learn how to deal with the more complicated conflict of intensity three.
6. Groups and teams who are emotionally unprepared to deal with complex and ambiguous situations can be discovered, and the spiritual and emotional growth issues of group interaction can be addressed.
7. Complex issues between groups and teams may actually be resolved in a manner such that they may not resurface in future years.

What Can Go Wrong at Intensity Three?

1. Groups or teams can fail to engage with their full heart, soul, mind, and strength. They can hold something back because they do not have the emotional maturity to handle intensity three conflict situations, or because they have decided they want to win and fully engaging may mean they will lose.
2. Without full, clear, and genuine trust, reasonable and true solutions may not occur.
3. Since groups or teams may fail to fully engage, the hoped for learnings from the experience may not occur, and the potential benefit for later intensity three conflicts may not exist.
4. The opportunity will be lost for deeper, more meaningful relationships that can result from people being involved in healthy, yet complicated, conflict situations.
5. The dialogue may not achieve resolution, and participants walk away realizing they are going to face these same groups or teams in a similar situation again.
6. Some participants engage in bad behavior during the dialogue around issues, relationships, and causes, creating an ongoing divide in the relationships and perhaps an escalation of the conflict.
7. The empowerment that could have been possible if collaboration or mediation had worked is lost for now, and perhaps forever.

Every Congregation Needs Intensity Three Conflict Situations

Intensity three conflict situations are potentially empowering to congregations. They represent great opportunities for groups and teams to learn how to handle complex conflict situations. At intensity three, skills can be developed in dealing with major challenges congregations must face to move in the direction of their full Kingdom potential.

Intensity three conflict situations are the last intensity in the list that congregations may be able to handle without third-party assistance, though sometimes they will need outside help. They will test the congregational leadership's ability to collaborate with people within their congregation who have differing values and goals concerning the future of the congregation, but who potentially can all unite under one vision.

The key learning is that every congregation needs intensity three conflict situations.

A Congregation Who Handled Intensity Three Conflict Well

In spite of repeated efforts by the pastor and the personnel committee of Holy Trinity, a conflict between the youth minister and the music minister could not be resolved. It was now impacting the entire staff and the personnel committee in a way that had moved beyond a conflict between two people to a conflict within the staff, within the personnel committee, and between the staff and personnel committee.

Next would be the congregation as a whole. However, all participants in the conflict were committed to not letting this conflict impact the great sense of ministry and Christian community in the congregation. This commitment included the music minister and the youth minister, who had conflict in their leadership styles, music styles, facilities space use, and theology.

After prayerful dialogue in a meeting of all participants, it was decided a mediator would be brought in to help work through their situation. A mediator was secured and met multiple times with the staff and personnel committee over a period of about ninety days. All possible issues were resolved. A few remained unresolved.

These unresolved issues primarily focused around the music minister being unwilling to trust the youth minister and the larger group. Having been present in the congregation for eight years, and, with several family transitions that were imminent, she volunteered to seek another place of service.

While both wins and losses were experienced, the best possible solutions were achieved based on the depth of willingness of the participants to collaborate and respond positively to mediation. The vast majority of the congregation never knew of this conflict. The music minister moved on to another congregation without negative incident.

COACHING INSIGHTS

■ Before reading this chapter, how did you handle intensity three conflicts? Could you correctly diagnose them, or did you become confused with causes being expressed for which the individual task-oriented and person-orientated issues were unclear?

■ What has gone right in the way you have handled intensity three conflicts in your congregation? What has gone wrong? What would you do differently?

■ If you are the pastor, a staff minister, or a program staff member, what have you learned about leading and managing conflict as you have addressed intensity three conflict situations? What are examples of how you have appropriately involved others in dealing with intensity three conflict situations?

■ How would you define solution or resolution of conflict at intensity three? When is it over? When is it likely to come up again? How can you tell the difference, and what might you do at the time to address this?

■ To what extent do you accept the fact that you must engage intensity three conflict situations and no longer have the opportunity to avoid them or to accommodate solutions someone else proposes?

■ What reasons do you believe support the premise that every congregation needs intensity three conflict situations? What can be learned from these situations that may empower the future life and ministry of your congregation? How can you share these learning throughout your congregation and thus increase your capacity to handle conflict situations?

PERSONAL REFLECTIONS

Your Reflections: What are your reflections on the material presented in this chapter?

_____

_____

_____

_____

_____

Your Actions: What actions do you need to take about your life, ministry, and/or congregation based on the material presented in this chapter?

_____

_____

_____

_____

_____

Your Accountability: How and by whom do you want to be held accountable for taking these actions?

_____

_____

_____

_____

_____

5

The Fourth Intensity of Conflict

Now It's Time to Vote or Else

EXECUTIVE SUMMARY

The purpose of this chapter is to dialogue about the fourth intensity of conflict, in which the causes of conflict now begin to become known throughout the active congregation. The focus will be on helping congregations engage the conflict rather than to deny it so that the conflict may be mediated during a time before the conflict becomes unhealthy. Various methods of voting will emerge during this level of intensity. They provide a key to understanding the impact of the conflict on the congregation. This level of intensity frequently becomes a highly organized win-lose situation in which the importance of winning becomes very important to the people of at least one major perspective on the conflict situation.

Image of Intensity Four Conflict

Intensity four conflict involves the potential for change in the river valley. It is raining in the mountains, but it is not raining in the valley. People from the east side of the river were headed for a hunting trip in the mountains and were turned away by the severity of the storms as they approached the mountains. Based on reports they received from local people in the mountains, it would appear this is the biggest storm they have seen in more than thirty years. They remember that the last time there was this much rain the valley flooded.

With this is mind, when the hunters return home, they share with their friends and neighbors on the east side of the river their information about the storms and the potential for flooding. The communities on the east and west side of the river have both developed during the past twenty-seven years. Other than being required to purchase flood insurance because they are in a 100-year flood plain, they know nothing about the potential for destruction from immediate flooding.

The community on the east side of the river decides to organize an effort to sandbag their side of the river. They also choose not to share information about the rain and potential flooding with the people on the west side of the river. They have never gotten along well with those people anyway.

Over the next twenty-four hours, as the citizens build a sandbag barrier on the east side of the river, the people on the west side observe what is happening. They send a representative of the west river community over to the east side to ask what is going on. When told of the potential flooding, she hurries back to the west side to tell her friends and neighbors about the imminent flooding. But it is too late. Within a few hours the water begins to rise in the community. Flooding appears inevitable.

Overview of Intensity Four Conflict

No congregation needs intensity four conflict situations.

Intensity four conflict shifts from a competition within a group or between groups in a congregation to a congregation-wide competition with voting. Like intensity three, it is a win-lose situation. Each side not only wants to win, but feels an urgency to win. They devote significant time to organizing their effort to win.

A congregation-wide competition can be defined numerically. If 20 to 25 percent of the average number of active attending adults are aware of the various identifiable causes and some of the issues, and have taken a side in a conflict, then it is a congregation-wide, intensity four conflict situation. This does not mean 20 to 25 percent on each aside. It means between the two sides together are a total of 20 to 25 percent of the congregation involved. The majority of the active congregation, in a medium size or larger congregation, may not be very aware of the conflict. They particularly may not know a great deal about the issues and people who are involved.

It does not take much effort, particularly in smaller membership congregations with less than eighty to eighty-five people in average attendance, to create a congregation-wide competition. It is a very short walk from a few people being in conflict to 20 percent of the active congregation being in conflict. It is one of the issues that hinder these congregations from having healthy, functional, nonanxious congregational life. It also hinders them from growing beyond eighty–to–eighty-five people in attendance if that is both their goal and their potential.

Intensity four conflict situations represent a transitional intensity between healthy conflict and unhealthy conflict. They are difficult to manage and may escalate if not managed appropriately and fairly quickly. In many situations, emotion has taken over. Participants in the conflict are no longer functioning based primarily on principles and Christ-centered core values. They are functioning on the basis of cultural positions that overrule a principled approach.

Often at this conflict intensity various participants are seeking to secure the support of people outside the congregation. One or both sides will contact denominational representatives, or other persons with influence on the life of the congregation. Particularly when the polity of the denomination is connectional, persons with authority concerning the affairs of the congregation or the placement of the clergy will be approached to join one side or the other in the conflict.

Former pastors and members who may have been involved in previous conflicts of a similar nature in the congregation will be approached as trusted truth tellers who can provide perceived truthful information concerning some of the issues surrounding the various causes. Often their truth is subjective information that further blurs the situation. Their support generally is not sought so truth could be provided. It is sought so one cause or the other can be justified.

At least one side at intensity four is preparing to take the conflict to intensity five. They feel this may be necessary to win. At times the second side is not making such preparations because they do not understand the intensity as being that serious. They are not people who desire to fight at the next intensity. They think the first side will eventually come around and agree to a positive way forward.

The tendencies of an intensity three conflict have now become urgencies at intensity four. For example, people are urged to choose a side in the conflict. Language is very general and often accusatory, and does not share helpful, clarifying information. People attack one another with their words, and urge others to join them in the attacks. Participants on opposite sides of the conflict are unable to talk to one another in a gracious manner, if at all. They avoid one another.

Prayer becomes more urgent. People pray to God for a sign or a clear indication of direction for taking action on the conflict. They think they know what action to take against the other side in the conflict, but they yearn for heavenly affirmation.

Voting becomes part of the process at intensity four. Formal voting is done by the elders, board, or congregation, depending on the governance system of the congregation. Multiple types of voting occur, and most are not directly related to the formal governance system.

At least seven ways exist in which people vote. People vote with their hands or ballots in board or congregational meetings. People vote with their wallet or pocketbooks by the giving or withholding of their tithes and offerings. People vote with their feet by their presence (or lack thereof) in worship and program activities of the congregation. People vote with their time by volunteering for leadership roles in the congregation, refusing to accept new leadership roles, or resigning from roles they currently fulfill. People vote with their mouths by speaking well of their congregation, or by speaking with negative criticism concerning their congregation. People vote with their zeal by encouraging people to connect with the congregation or by discouraging people to connect. People vote with their prayers by praying earnestly that love might abound within their congregation, or failing to pray in earnest for their congregation.

Often at intensity four the presenting issues are not the core issues. It is even possible the core issues may have been forgotten by many people engaged in the conflict. Some people will not even have gotten involved in the conflict until after clarity around the core issues has become lost in the midst of debates surrounding various causes. These people may be clueless about the core or initiating issues. To the extent they become leaders in the various causes, they cannot deal with the core issues because they were not involved when they developed, and do not know what they are. If they ever understand the core issue or issues, they may actually lose their zeal for the current conflict.

A very important point to remember about the actions of groups during intensity four conflict situations is that for many of them the good of the congregation is more important than winning. Winning is definitely important. However, they will stop trying to win if they perceive that winning would do permanent damage to the congregation.

Examples of the types of causes that rise to an intensity four conflict situation include, but are not limited to the following:

1. Calling a new pastor, or having such a pastor appointed or placed in the congregation, who possesses a theology, style of ministry, or personality that will significantly change the direction of the congregation.
2. Discussions on making a major change in the affiliation of the congregation with its denomination over theological or moral issues, for which there is not unity in the congregation on the same issues.
3. Cost overruns on a major building project for which adequate funding is not available, and it appears some leaders have known about this for a while and did not share it with the congregation.
4. Worship wars around a new worship service and/or the elimination of an old service loved by a certain percentage of the congregation.
5. Major disagreements over the emerging philosophy and style of ministry advocated by a new pastor, staff, and new lay members of the congregation that will change the basic character and nature of the congregation.
6. The fear of longer-tenured members that they are losing control of the congregation to newer, younger members in a way the longer-tenured members see as detrimental to their future perspective on the congregation.
7. In smaller membership congregations, fights between the core families of the congregation that are primarily taking place in the community, but spill over into the congregation.

Congregational Illustrations of Intensity Four

Staff and Worship Conflict in Good Shepherd Church

Intensity four conflict occurs when the board gets involved in the debate about worship and who should be considered the key leader of worship. From the perspective of some leaders, the music director and the pastor should have worked through this issue long ago. But they did not.

By this point, most of the active participants in the congregation are aware that a worship war is going on in the congregation. Much of the congregation is disappointed at the manner in which the pastor and music director are conducting themselves. At the same time, people begin to line up in support of one or the other.

It is proposed this may be the time to have two worship services. One could be a traditional liturgical service, and the other one would be a praise service. In doing this the music at the traditional, liturgical worship service can match that service, and the sermon at the praise service can be more interactive and dialogical.

The difficulty is the music director refuses to do the type of music wanted at the traditional, liturgical worship service, and the pastor says he does not know how to do an interactive, dialogical sermon. The church is at an impasse. A vote of the board is eminent. The whole active congregation is watching.

Leadership vs. Management in Trinity Church

Intensity four conflict develops when the conflict with the finance committee moves to a congregation-wide intensity. The number of people who have taken sides on the conflict becomes greater than 20 to 25 percent of the active participants. Members of the finance committee have figuratively bowed their backs in opposition to attempts to make them affirm projects with which they do not agree. They put together a list of what they call financial waste, particularly by the pastor and church staff, and share it throughout the congregation.

Many older adults support the members of the finance committee because they believe their financial conservatism is important for the long-term health of the congregation. The pastor and numerous people associated with the vision fulfillment leadership community continue to oppose the actions of the finance committee and request they be replaced with more cooperative persons. Somewhere along the way the HVAC issue got lost. It is no longer being raised.

In some cases congregational participants have started withholding their tithes and offerings from the congregation due to the accusations of financial irregularities and waste. Still, the controversy has not yet significantly impacted the attendance in this congregation.

A congregational business meeting is ultimately called to determine the authority lines over finances. By almost a two-thirds vote the congregation decides the pastor and board have the authority to tell the finance committee what items are approved for funding. The role of the finance committee is to make the funds available for the priorities of the congregation to the extent they are available from appropriate revenue streams or reserve funds. At the conclusion of the meeting four members of the finance committee announce they are leaving the congregation. Upon hearing this, the congregation applauds.

Women's Bible Study Group in Grace Church

Intensity four conflict blossoms when dialogue over the biblical perspective of various curricula used in the congregation has grown into a debate over the right theological position of the congregation and whether or not the teaching, preaching, and music has the correct biblical perspective. People are beginning to ask what type of congregation they are becoming.

Emily and Kim's Bible study group long ago chose a curriculum, worked through their discussion over the curriculum, and kept most of the study group together. Several women left the group and became part of the ongoing debate in the congregation over its theological stance.

Many people in the congregation have little or no idea about the debate going on over the Bible and the theological perspective of the congregation. Enough do, however, to raise the intensity of congregation discussion so that it can be called a congregation-wide competition.

Addressing Intensity Four Conflict

"Getting Past No!" is the theme of intensity four conflict. The natural tendency is to have a vote that firmly and formally rejects and marginalizes one side in the conflict. The goal of addressing intensity four conflict situations is to move past a negative vote to see if there is a positive solution many people can embrace.

The use of a third party from outside the congregation is needed to address this intensity, but often it is not sought soon enough. At times this third party is brought in to mediate dialogue between various factions and causes in the conflict. At other times this outside intervention is brought in to moderate a business session of the board or the congregation.

Because the possibility exists that participants—even in an intensity four conflict situation—want a solution, first attempt to achieve a collaborative solution. Seek to identify intensity one, two, and three conflict issues and causes that have become part of this intensity four conflict situation. This will take some concentrated work, but it can be done.

Once identified, then seek to have them assessed according to their own merit. The urgency will be to see the interconnectedness of everything and indicate each individual issue is so tied into the larger issue that they cannot stand on their own merit. Resist this urgency. Often specific issues, procedures, and perspectives can be separated from the larger issue and dealt with at a lower intensity of conflict. Over time, without the individual issues attached to a larger cause, the larger cause may not seem so unmanageable.

At the same time collaborative solutions are being sought, the third party that is brought in should be prepared to shift to a negotiation stance in which wins and losses are identified. This will be necessary when one or both sides are unable to dialogue about solutions that go beyond the positions they are taking on the issues and causes. They may be so entrenched that a negotiated settlement is the best that can result from an intensity four conflict situation.

Methods to use at intensity four are the development of consensus issue statements, ground rules for fair conflict engagement, and trust development among the participants. Help each side see how they have contributed to the current conflict, and how they can contribute to the desired solution. When these methods are not working in a situation in which a collaborative solution is being sought, it is an indication of the need to shift to a negotiation style.

Participants, with the assistance of the third-party conflict mediator, should identify the prime core values held throughout the congregation that unite them around a sense of overall mission. These prime core values could, and perhaps should, supersede any collection of issues or causes in a congregation. Many congregations have only a few such values. These values will affirm the active participation of God in the past, present, and future ministry of the congregation.

Also identify goals held by various participants that are superseded by these prime core values. Such goals may be negotiable for many participants based on the principle that the good of the congregation is more important that winning.

If it appears winning is more important to either or both sides in the conflict than is the health and well-being of the congregation, this may actually be a sign of intensity five conflict and efforts to mediate the conflict should be rethought as inadequate.

Perceived Truthful Information

At intensity four conflict a new type of information begins to be prominent. It has existed at lower intensities of conflict, but it is being fully expressed beginning at intensity four. It is called *perceived truthful information*. Throughout intensities one and two conflict, it was always possible to discern and discover the factual truth. Beginning with intensity three that becomes improbable.

This fact is illustrated by the image at the beginning of chapter 4 of someone sticking a hand in a river seeking to determine the source or stream from which the water his or her hand is touching came. At intensity three, because individual issues have combined into concerns or causes, identifying the original, individual issues becomes improbable—not impossible, just improbable. At intensity four it is impossible.

What takes the place of specific truth is *perceived truthful information* that is sometimes a general body of information, but often a collection of subjective perceptions that are partially based in fact, but are not themselves factual. It is like circumstantial evidence in a court of law that never quite establishes guilt or innocence.

Perceived truthful information is more powerful than truth. It is what people come to believe to be truth. It fits their preconceived notions. It fits their position on the conflict situation. They convince themselves and others that it is truth.

Perceived truthful information is not substantive truth. It is a combination of some truth plus attitudes and emotions. It is often based in *some* facts, but becomes a sort of half-truth. It is filtered through cultural, ideological, and psychological filters and becomes truth to those who proclaim it as truth.

People captivated by *perceived truthful information* may even be unable to accept factual truth when it is presented to them. They have become convinced they know the truth. Intensity four conflict situations cannot, therefore, be mediated based solely on truth. They must take into account the power of *perceived truthful information,* and the control it has on some people involved in the conflict.

COACHING BREAK

✔ Gaze out the window for a minute. Ponder the situation of your congregation. What images come to mind?

✔ Are there examples of intensity four conflicts that occasionally arise in the life and ministry of your congregation? How does your congregation handle these issues? How are you able to keep these conflicts focused on the good of the congregation rather than winning the cause?

✔ As you think about your experience with intensity four issues, ask yourself if you were able to focus on "Getting Past *No!*" and to not allow the conflict to escalate to the next, higher unhealthy intensity.

✔ Did you bring in outside, third-party leadership? If so, when? Where did you find this leadership? Was the outside assistance in time to help, or too late to keep the conflict from escalating?

✔ What role has *perceived truthful information* played in intensity four conflicts? What ways have you found to discern and discover the truth, and to help people overcome their tendencies to believe perceptions rather than the truth?

What Can Go Right at Intensity Four?

1. Mediation can work.
2. The good of the congregation wins as the primary motive of the conflict participants, and they find a way to de-escalate the conflict.
3. Participants are able to distinguish between perceived truthful information and actual truth, thus providing a solid starting point for mediation.
4. Voting takes place only around process issues that help mediate the conflict situation.
5. A desire to live into the prime core values of the congregation causes participants to determine their causes of conflict are less important than these core values.
6. Many leaders can learn how to work their way through this transitional intensity of conflict with the help of an outside third party.
7. New leaders emerge who act as statespersons and successfully call on the congregation to rise above its potential unhealthy conflict.

What Can Go Wrong at Intensity Four?

1. Mediation can fail.
2. The emotional tension is so great that winning becomes everything and the conflict escalates to an intensity five.

3. Perceived truthful information becomes so powerful that it overwhelms any attempts to seek actual truth.
4. Votes take place that further divide the congregation into two opposing sides.
5. Participants argue over the rightness of prime core values to the point they become meaningless statements of idealistic desires.
6. The services of an outside third party are rejected.
7. A failure of leadership from clergy and laity is experienced, and the conflict escalates to intensity five, in which some of the leaders are forced to leave the congregation.

No Congregation Needs Intensity Four Conflict Situations

Every congregation, unfortunately, will from time to time experience intensity four conflict situations, even though no one *needs* them. When they occur, they test the courage of congregational leaders to step forward and seek to provide a way forward through a difficult set of circumstances.

The tensions of intensity four conflict situations begin to deter congregations from their primarily spiritual, missional, and fellowship roles. Strategic processes, growth emphases, and spiritual disciple-making processes all tend to stop, waiting to see what the outcomes and impacts of the conflict situation will be.

While every congregation needs a little conflict, no congregation really needs intensity four conflicts.

Congregations Who Handled Intensity Four Conflict by Finding a Way Forward

Woodhaven and Patterson are congregations who both had a founding pastor crisis. In each case the founding pastor had been present for more than twenty years. As is typical, both love and dislike are expressed for founding pastors after many years of service.

A founding pastor owns and feels some depth of accountability for many, if not all, areas of a congregation. With this comes the tendency of congregational members to blame the founding pastor when things begin to wane in the congregational vitality toward the end of the first generation of congregational life.

Opposition to the pastor is often expressed by the beginning of the third decade of congregational life. The reaction of the pastor to this opposition is critical. A good reaction generally promotes a healthy process. A bad reaction can lead to an unhealthy process. In either case, at intensity four this conflict is a congregation-wide movement.

The pastor of Woodhaven was deeply hurt by the expressed and implied opposition of intensity four conflict. At the same time, she saw the value in seeing the current conflict as typical and something the congregation could handle with outside assistance. Early during this intensity four conflict, she approached her governing board about securing the services of a conflict management consultant. They agreed, and the congregation concurred in a called business session.

The process was well engaged by the congregation under the leadership of the consultant. The pastor had both strengths and weaknesses. Some of her weaknesses in administration had shown up more as the congregation had grown larger. Finances were strained not only because of the conflict, but because of the economic direction of the area in which the church was located.

The outcome was that the pastor was able to remain another ten years until retirement. A small vocal group in the congregation refused to accept the reality of the perspective presented to the congregation by the consultant. They left the church, but not before making some accusations against various people that cemented in the minds of the remaining congregation that it was a good thing they left.

Because of this conflict, Woodhaven may not have thrived as well as was their potential. They did, however, enjoy quality ministry over the next decade with the leadership of the founding pastor.

Patterson, on the other hand, had multiple people who engaged in emotionally immature actions, others who engaged in conflict avoidance, and many who were passive aggressive in their actions. The founding pastor was smothering the congregation with his leadership actions. The congregation was ready to move on to a second generation of life.

Realizing he was being criticized in many areas of his life and ministry, the founding pastor sought to deflect the criticism by blaming the issues on various staff persons. He was able, over an eighteen-month period, to force out two staff ministers in the hope that would save him. The thought that he was the problem was totally alien to his perspective.

Rather than engaging this intensity four conflict early, this situation continued for a long time without outside assistance.

By the time a consultant was brought in, the conflict was almost at intensity five, at which point the congregation might publicly fire the pastor.

Perceived truthful information was rampant throughout the congregation. It was difficult for anyone to clearly discover core truth. The pastor was adamant his leadership was the appropriate leadership. Various laypersons were entrenched in their positions on the pastor and the future of the congregation. It was really a situation in which everyone was beginning to wonder if winning—for some people, including the pastor—was more important than the good of the congregation.

The consultant made an interesting recommendation. He did not feel the pastor had done anything illegal, immoral, or unethical that required his removal from the congregation. At the same time, it appeared the confidence of the congregation in the pastor had diminished to the point that he could not serve the congregation with effectiveness. Therefore, the pastor needed to leave.

The congregation was not without sin or wrong. It had drifted into a position at which it was no longer clear on its spiritual strategic direction and fought over many issues. Even the consultant did not feel the need for the congregation to go back and correct past corporate wrongs. It needed to find a way forward. A process of healing and reconciliation followed by a spiritual strategic journey was recommended.

The congregation embraced all the recommendations. The pastor's tenure was brought to a close. The congregation called an interim pastor. They began work within 120 days on a new spiritual strategic direction. That has now been more than fifteen years ago. The congregation has great vitality and has weathered numerous typical crises while also making great Kingdom progress.

COACHING INSIGHTS

- Before reading this chapter, how did you handle intensity four conflicts, if you had them? Could you correctly diagnose them, or did you become entangled in this intensity of conflict and forget it really could be positively addressed?

- What has gone right in the way you have handled intensity four conflicts in your congregation? What has gone wrong? What would you do differently?

■ If you are the pastor, a staff minister, or a program staff member, what have you learned about leading and managing conflict as you have addressed intensity four conflict situations? What are examples of how you have appropriately involved others in dealing with intensity four conflict situations?

■ How would you define solution or resolution of conflict at intensity four? Is resolution even possible at intensity four? If so, under what circumstances can it occur?

■ Why is it impossible to ignore intensity four conflicts? Why are clergy and laity inside congregations experiencing intensity four conflicts unable to handle them? Why do they wait so long to ask for outside, third-party assistance?

■ Are you clear on why no congregation needs intensity four conflicts? What, if any, good can come from an intensity four conflict situation?

PERSONAL REFLECTIONS

Your Reflections: What are your reflections on the material presented in this chapter?

_____

_____

_____

_____

_____

Your Actions: What actions do you need to take about your life, ministry, and/or congregation based on the material presented in this chapter?

_____

_____

_____

_____

_____

Your Accountability: How and by whom do you want to be held accountable for taking these actions?

_____

_____

_____

_____

_____

6

The Fifth Intensity of Conflict
Dividing the Medes from the Persians

EXECUTIVE SUMMARY

The purpose of this chapter is to dialogue about the fifth intensity of conflict, in which the mandate arises to terminate the pastor, force the losers to leave the congregation, or both. The focus will be on helping congregations who experience the organizational casualties of this intensity of conflict face the implications of their actions, and figure out how to renew a foundation for future life as a Christ-centered, faith-based community. The level of intensity really involves losing and leaving. No one wins.

Image of Intensity Five

Intensity five conflict is experienced through the rising water and the flooding on the west side of the valley. Some water flows into low places on the east side, but major flooding occurs on the west side to the extent people have to leave their homes. The east side was prepared. The west side was not. The east side knew of the possibility of flooding. The west side did not until it was too late.

People in the community are displaced. Particularly on the west side of the river, people have to evacuate their homes. People on the east side of the river experience some flooding, but no one has to evacuate their homes. Some of the east side residents feel remorse over not sharing the news of the imminent flooding with the people on the west side of the river. Others on the east side say they simply need to clean up the mess the flooding made on their side of the river and move on with their lives.

Overview of Intensity Five

No congregation deserves intensity five conflict situations.

Intensity five conflicts are congregation-wide combat situations, with organizational casualties. It is a lose-leave situation in which senior pastors and staff ministers are terminated, and churches separate or split into two or more congregations. In biblical terms, it divides the "Medes" from the "Persians."

The urgency for all key congregational leaders to identify themselves with one cause or another has now become a mandate at intensity five. If leaders do not identify themselves with one cause or another, they will be given an identity by one or more of the causes as being on the other side. It is impossible for leaders to remain neutral at intensity five. Leaders cannot work with both sides any more. They will be rejected.

Thus, intensity five conflicts have a heavy dose of focus on the person and the position of the congregational pastor. Even if the pastor was not the primary cause of any of the major issues of conflict, and even if the pastor was not a leader of one of the identified causes of conflict, the pastor at intensity five conflicts is one of the key issues, if not the key issue. The pastor is demonized by some, and awarded sainthood by others or seen as a victim of the demonizing.

Direct attempts are frequently made to terminate the pastor. Often these attempts do not follow a formal governance approach, but rather rise from informal pressure placed on the pastor to resign. Too often these efforts are successful. At times the polity or governance system of a denomination requires the congregational control groups who want the pastor gone to work through denominational hierarchy. When this is the case, the conflict spreads to a broader arena.

If and when the pastor leaves, several other things may happen. First, leaders of the cause that got rid of the pastor rejoice. They then declare the problem is gone or has been eliminated and the church simply needs to get a new pastor and move on with congregational life. They try to ignore the existence of various lingering outputs and impacts of the conflict situation.

Second, others leave the congregation either because they were supporters of the pastor, or because they are frustrated with the conflict situation and its impact on their spiritual and emotional feeling about this congregation. Some of these people scatter to various congregations, some join a new congregation that may separate or split from the congregation, and some give up on church for at least a while.

Third, the terminated pastor may lead a group a people to go out from the congregation and start a new congregation. In many cases this is a nasty split with strong emotions between the two congregations that last for many years. In some cases it is a mutually agreed upon separation that both the old congregation and the new congregation affirm. In either case it is an unfortunate result, but one that may not be avoided at intensity five conflict.

Generally, the remaining congregation is just glad the former pastor and supporters of the pastor have left. They may even speak good words about the pastor and new congregation to those who ask. They may also champion the new congregation to their denomination.

A very important point to remember about the actions of groups during intensity five conflict situations is that for many winning has now become more important than the good of the congregation. Winning is now essential. If the congregation is permanently damaged, that is unfortunate, but necessary, from the perspective of the conflict antagonists. The thought even exists among a few that they are carrying out God's will or God's orders to get rid of the evil ones who are hurting this congregation.

Some laity approach this as a business decision. The pastor no longer has the confidence of the congregation, so the pastor must leave. This business approach may be addressing the inevitable in some situations. In others it is ignoring the spiritual and emotional differences between a business organization and a congregation, and the lingering impact on the congregation for many years into the future.

Intensity five conflict situations can also have an opposite outcome. The pastor can mount a defense against the attack made on him, and can at times win. More often than not, this is a short-term win. A pastor with a strong, proactive leadership style may be able to organize against the opposition and force votes and other actions that cause the opposition to the pastor to back down, withdraw from the congregation, or separate out to form a new congregation.

It can happen that laypersons who support the pastor in these counter-offensives are doing so because they are opposed to other laypersons who are trying to terminate the pastor. Once the laypersons attacking the pastor have withdrawn, it is possible these apparent supporters of the pastor may still seek to get rid of the pastor within six-to-eighteen months.

Another twist on intensity five conflict situations focused on the pastor is that, at first, opposition laypersons may seek to terminate an offending staff person. They may do this to test their ability to later terminate the pastor. They may also do this because they hope the performance of the pastor might improve if a weak staff person is replaced with a strong staff person. Often this is only a delaying strategy for the inevitable.

Pastors who fear for their ministry position and their ministry career and reputation may be enablers of the strategy to terminate a staff member. They may offer to help terminate the staff person in the hope they will not be next. This is only a delaying tactic, and suggests some interesting observations about the integrity of the pastor.

To recap, the objectives at intensity five change from wanting to win to wanting to hurt and/or get rid of the others. At this intensity it is no longer believed the other cause participants can or will change. Therefore, it is believed the only choice is removal of them from the congregation. Being right and punishing become predominate themes. Clear lines mark who is in and who is out of each of the causes. Strong leaders emerge, and members of factions conform to the wishes of the leaders, and the will of the cause.

The language used in the conflict jells into ideology. Members of factions talk about non-negotiable convictions more than issues. They refer to convictions such as truth, freedom, justice, and the will and Word of God.

If people are still praying at intensity five, it may be prayers such as, "Lord, thank you that this is your will. I did what was necessary. It was and is still painful. Can we leave it alone, and move forward?" They may also earnestly pray for the people who were forced to leave the congregation since they wish them no long-term harm. They just wanted them to leave so the congregation could move forward with like-minded persons in leadership and management.

Examples of the types of causes that rise to an intensity five conflict situation include, but are not limited to the following:

1. Major issues focused upon the pastor and staff regarding their performance, their personality and relationship ability, or moral or legal difficulties.
2. Major efforts at control by various sub-groups within the church that are pushed until they become major conflicts.
3. Immorality or legal difficulties on the part of a major, visible lay leader, in which the congregation is unable to handle disciplining this respected leader and the conflict escalates to intensity five.
4. Controversy over a moral and ethical issue with competing biblical viewpoints such as homosexuality, abortion, genetic engineering, the role of women in ministry, or addictions of various kinds.
5. The inability of the congregation to adequately deal with intensity four conflicts that get out of hand and escalate to intensity five for reasons no one may be able to explain.
6. Theological controversies, perhaps tied to denominational conflicts, that divide the congregation over what are considered core doctrinal positions.
7. Diversity of theology, socioeconomics, education, worship style, and other similar issues that are too great for unity to be sustained in the congregation.

Congregational Illustrations of Intensity Five
Staff and Worship Conflict in Good Shepherd Church

Intensity five conflict develops when the worship war and conflict between the music director and the pastor results in one or both of them leaving the congregation. As the situation approaches this intensity, the music director's wife announces that she is leaving him and their two children to pursue a life of her own choosing with more fun, freedom, and less restrictions.

The music director resigns out of embarrassment. In figuring out how to raise his two daughters, ages four and seven, he decides to move 175 miles away to his hometown to be near his parents, who have offered to help with the granddaughters. Supporters of the music director initiate an argument over the pastor's lack of leadership. They contact the bishop through the pastor-parish relations committee to request he be appointed to another congregation.

The chairperson of the conference's $10 million capital fundraising campaign for church planting and congregational redevelopment is a member of this congregation and wants the pastor to leave. The bishop agrees to reappoint the pastor at the next opportunity.

The congregation denies that anything surrounding the conflict and the leaving of the two ministers was their fault. As a result, they do not deal with the circumstances that led them to allow conflict between two staff members escalate into an intensity five conflict. The bishop simply appoints a new pastor to their congregation. Three years later their lay leadership once again calls the bishop to ask that their pastor be reappointed. Their conflict intensity is again at five. This time the bishop refuses to appoint a new permanent pastor until they go through a conflict management process.

Leadership vs. Management in Trinity Church

Intensity five conflict arises when the congregation splits over the finances and authority fight. The members of the finance committee keep their promise, and fourteen families leave the congregation. Most of these families join another congregation in the same general area. Since a majority of these families had been significant financial contributors to the congregation, the church faces a real financial crisis. Now no funds are available to address the new high priority initiatives resulting from the vision fulfillment storytelling process.

The remaining congregation is depressed and calls in a pastoral counselor who specializes in healing reconciliation in congregations in conflict. Over a period of years the congregation slowly recovers from the conflict, develops a new base for moving forward in Kingdom ministry, and returns to the attendance and financial levels they had before the conflict arose. But it is now four years later, and they have missed the window of opportunity that once was present and open for them to soar to the next level and depth of Kingdom ministry.

Women's Bible Study Group in Grace Church

Intensity five conflict occurs when the congregation does one of the following things: On the one hand, the people who identify themselves as the more conservative people in the congregation believe the pastor is soft on the Bible and is not leading the congregation to have a deeply spiritual approach to worship and discipleship. They feel that if the pastor will not resign voluntarily, then they have to force him to leave, because, in their minds, the future spiritual foundation of the children and grandchildren in the congregation is at stake.

On the other hand, if the congregation *does* support the Bible as the inerrant Word of God, then a more moderate portion of the congregation feels they must leave to form a new congregation and ask the pastor to go out with them. The conservative side in the conflict indicates that if they do not win the fight, *they* are going as a group to join the congregation a mile or so further out from town that has a new pastor who is definitely a godly person.

One of these things will now happen for sure. In the process of moving to intensity five conflict, Kim's family, who had tried to stay neutral once the conflict spread throughout the congregation, decided they would have to leave the congregation if the pastor did not leave. Emily is mortified, and the relationship with Kim has become totally strained, with Kim hardly speaking to her any more.

At this intensity either the pastor is terminated, or the congregation is split into two congregations, with some groups of people moving on to another congregation in the area, not necessarily of the same denomination.

Addressing Intensity Five Conflict

"Getting to *Neutral!*" is the theme of intensity five conflict. The goal is to manage the conflict with the least possible damage to the congregation and its individual participants. It is not likely any attempts to manage an intensity five conflict situation will bring about resolution, or even an acceptable mediation of the conflict. The best that generally can be hoped for is the ability to stop the hemorrhaging and establish a new beginning point from which the congregation can move forward with healing and reconciliation, and the development of a new, positive future.

This is not the answer you wanted to hear. But it is generally the reality. You cannot be in denial at intensity five. Bad things are going to happen. You must acknowledge that neither you nor an outside third party is going to be able to work it out. People are going to leave. Permanent damage to the congregation is going to take place.

At intensity four there is still a lot of potential for mediation and negotiation between groups and causes. At intensity five an outside third party is brought in to divide the Medes from the Persians and to divide up the spoils of war. At times the entrance of a third party may be rejected by a group, or groups. Part of this is that the anger is severe. Part is that allowing a third party to enter the congregational system may mean their cause will not win. Or, for some people at intensity five, the end justifies the means, so they will oppose any interference from outside so they can manipulate the situation.

A rational response to intensity five will not work because emotion is out of control for at least the most identifiable antagonists. These antagonists will not allow the people following their lead to back down. The use of formal authority through voting and decisive decision-making is essential at this conflict intensity. Following clear, firm, enforceable ground rules is mandatory.

These ground rules may have to be introduced, required, and enforced by the third-party consultant or arbitrator. The third party may need these ground rules only for a specific decision-making session; or, if the third party is carrying out an extended process with the congregation, these ground rules may be needed for three to six months. After a lose-leave decision is made, allow for the withdrawal and separation of persons and groups motivated to leave. The outside third party may help the congregation complete the separation and set forth procedures for healing, reconciliation, and developing future ministry.

Completing the separation can include several areas of concern. First is the development of severance agreements for the pastor or staff members who are leaving. In some congregations these agreements must have the approval of the elders, a board, or the congregation itself. It is not unusual for the vote on severance to be the only formal vote surrounding the termination of a pastor or staff members.

Second can be the decision about the division of any liquid or hard assets. It might be thought that, if people leave voluntarily or are terminated, all assets remain with the existing congregation. However, this may not always be true. Claims on assets by people who are leaving may be legitimate. At intensity five the division of such assets can be worked out reasonably well. If not, the conflict intensity may escalate to intensity six.

Third, while it may seem like an unusual thing to occur, it is possible to negotiate, once the termination or separation has occurred, a covenant of relationship between the people who remain and the people who leave. This is particularly true if both sides in the conflict want to move forward with healing, reconciliation, and developing future ministry. It is difficult to dialogue about such a covenant immediately after the termination or separation. It is at times possible to do so within a few months.

Healing, reconciliation, and developing a future ministry plan are all proactive steps that can be very helpful to congregations following an intensity five conflict situation. The remaining congregation must engage in some intentional efforts to rebuild relationships with God, one another, and the context they serve. This must be both a spiritual and a relationship process. A great exercise for doing this, known as "Share and Prayer Triplets," is described in my book *Pursuing the Full Kingdom Potential of Your Congregation*, published by Chalice Press of St. Louis in 2006.

Briefly, this is a process of gathering groups of three people together. Members of each group have various perspectives on the conflict situation. Ask the groups to meet ten times for up to 100 minutes over a period of 100 days. As they gather, they have dialogue and prayer concerning the past, present, and future of their congregation. *All* the people involved in the triplets also gather together two or three times over the 100 days for dialogue and prayer as a larger group. The purpose is to build a new relational base from which a new future ministry plan can be developed.

Usually four to six months following an intensity five conflict situation, a congregation is ready to consider its new future. I often recommend congregations use a future storytelling process such as the one described in my book referenced above. This future storytelling process can take up to six months, at which time it would have about ten to twelve months since the major incidents of conflict. At that point the congregation may be ready for a new pastor. During the year after the conflict erupted at intensity five, the congregation should have an interim pastor.

Termination

Termination is a more complex issue than it may appear. Often pastors and staff members are terminated without the vote of any official congregational body. Pastors or staff members may come under such pressure that they resign, rather than being fired, to get relief from the stress they and their families are experiencing. Pastors or staff members may resign because of an informal or formal offer of an extended financial severance if they are willing to resign rather than forcing the congregation to go through the pain and loss that will be experienced through the process of firing them.

Moral or legal issues of which the pastor or staff members are guilty may be ready to be exposed, and the pastor or staff members are offered the opportunity to resign first. In a clergy appointment system, a pastor or staff minister may be appointed to a new congregation, and thus a congregational and denominational termination event is avoided.

Whatever the reason, in all of these cases no formal vote takes place to terminate the pastor or staff member. Still it is a termination. I have read studies and heard conversations among experts for decades that suggest a majority of pastor or staff member terminations never come to a vote by elders, the board, or the congregation. This reality probably still exists.

Repeat Offenders

Too often, congregations who experience an intensity five conflict become repeat offenders. These are congregations who return to an intensity five conflict occasionally, or with some regularity, because they do not deal with the issues in their congregational culture that caused their conflict to escalate to intensity five the first time.

The most important period for a congregation that has experienced intensity five conflict is the six to-eighteen months following an intensity five situation. Congregations typically have one of three types of reactions following intensity five. First, they may seek to deny the congregation has any remaining problems. The problems have left. The congregation needs to move forward. These congregations are destined to repeat their dysfunctional patterns of life. They may return to intensity five conflict within three to five years. They may even become repeat offenders and experience an intensity five conflict *every* three to five years. Only divine or significant human intervention can break these congregations out of this destructive pattern.

Second, they may acknowledge there are some minor problems related to the governance procedures of the congregation, which caused them to deal with the conflict issues in a negative way. However, changing the governance procedures and documents should handle this. Also, the position description and expectations of the pastor need to be modified so the congregation does not end up with a pastor like the last one. The long-term prognosis for these congregations is not much better than for those that deny there are any remaining problems. At minimum, these congregation go into a retirement mode, in which management and programs provide leadership for the congregation. It may not be as soon as three years, but within some short range of years these congregations may also experience another intensity five conflict situation. They will also need significant intervention to halt their cycle of dysfunction.

Third, the congregation may realize it has systemic problems and seek to address them. This is the healthiest response congregations can make. Those who acknowledge this can begin building a new foundation for ministry that may allow them never to return to intensity five conflict again. This is where processes of healing, reconciliation, and developing a future ministry plan are helpful.

COACHING BREAK

✔ Gaze out the window for a minute. Ponder the situation of your congregation. What images come to mind?

✔ What are examples of intensity five conflicts, if any, that have arisen in the life and ministry of your congregation? How does your congregation handle these issues?

✔ How are you able to keep these conflicts from becoming terminations or separation? If you haven't, how have you handled this disruption to congregational life?

✔ As you think back to your previous experience with intensity five conflicts (if any), ask yourself if you were able to focus on "Getting to *Neutral!*," or did losing take over as the mantra for the body life of your congregation? What role did an outside third party play in helping you manage your way through the intensity five conflict situation(s)?

What Can Go Right at Intensity Five?

1. Not much, because it is a painful time in the life of a congregation.
2. The presence of an outside third party who knows the art or science of his or her craft as a conflict manager can be of great assistance during a tough time.
3. The congregation that remains can realize this conflict was a great mistake and did much harm, and they can be committed to healing and reconciliation and to developing a new, positive ministry future.
4. This may seem odd, but the termination or separation is handled in a straightforward manner and not by manipulation behind the scenes.
5. Severance agreements, division of any appropriate assets, and development of a covenant between those who left and those who stayed are all processes that are handled well.
6. During any voting, individuals take personal responsibility for their votes, and they do not seek to just go along with the crowd.

7. Antagonists that remain in the congregation are marginalized by a new set of leaders who emerge to help the congregation build a more Christlike future.

What Can Go Wrong at Intensity Five?

1. The pain of this intensity conflict is incredible, and people are immobilized by it and drawn into making extremely unwise decisions.
2. The presence of an outside third party is not positive, and actually makes the situation worse because the congregation does not respond well to this intervention, the intervention is not done well, or both.
3. The congregation that remains denies there is anything systemically wrong with their congregation. They just want to move on to call a new pastor or to rebuild the congregation following their losses.
4. The termination or separation is handled in very manipulative ways by people who do not follow any ground rules except their own—that the end justifies the means.
5. Severance agreements, division of any appropriate assets, and development of a covenant between those who left and those who stayed are all processes that are handled badly and create secondary conflicts.
6. During any voting, people vote as a mob and refuse to take any personal responsibility for the outcome.
7. Antagonists who remain in the congregation take full control of the congregation and continue unhealthy and dysfunctional patterns of relating to God, one another, and the context of the congregation.

No Congregation Deserves Intensity Five Conflict Situations

Many congregations, unfortunately, will experience intensity five conflicts. When they occur, it is hoped some type of repentance and restoration can eventually take place in the life and ministry of the congregation. If not, the congregation may move to becoming a cultural enclave rather than a Christ-centered, faith-based community.

No sense of Kingdom ministry is possible in intensity five conflict situations. No congregation who periodically experiences intensity five can reach its full Kingdom potential. Strategic processes, growth emphases, and spiritual disciple-making processes all are sidelined or derailed at this intensity.

While every congregation needs a little conflict, no congregation really needs intensity five conflicts.

A Congregation Who Worked through a Termination and Addressed Repeat Offenders

Harrison Memorial was more than three decades old when it reached a crisis point with its pastor, who had been present for less than four years. Several lay leaders plotted to use their formal positions and charter membership in the congregation to force the early retirement of this pastor, whom they evaluated as ineffective.

The pastor saw it coming. When confronted in a meeting with a request to resign, he asked for a continuance in the meeting to think about their request for a couple of days. Four days later when the meeting reconvened, he walked in the room with his attorney. He said he would not leave and was prepared to take legal action against the congregation if they sought to force his resignation.

While at first this might appear to be an intensity six conflict situation, in reality it was a five because the presence of the attorney was a show of force rather than a solid plan for legal action. Both sides backed down, and a conflict management consultant was secured.

The congregation had peaked in numerical growth. They had needed to keep growing to pay for a new sanctuary, other additions, and renovations to existing facilities. Under this pastor they had declined in attendance and diminished in finances. They were having difficulty making their debt payments and engaging in essential programs and ministries.

Several lay leaders far exceeded their authority and common sense in thinking they had the power and support of the congregation to terminate the pastor. The pastor, on the other hand, did not appear to be up to the challenge of this congregation. While he was a good pastor, the context and situation of the congregation called for an exceptional pastor.

The consultant indicated the congregation had sinned against the pastor by suggesting to him they needed someone who would focus on care and community. What they really wanted was someone who would grow the attendance and increase the finances. The former agenda was verbalized to the pastor by the pastor search committee. The latter was the agenda of the charter members and their supporters.

In his report, the consultant recommended the pastor leave. The bond between pastor and congregation had been broken along the way. The consultant also indicated the congregation needed to accept much of the blame for the pastor needing to leave, because they had an agenda hidden from the pastor before he was called to the church. He further recommended several charter members give up some roles they had played since the founding of the congregation and that they not be eligible to be reelected or reappointed to these roles. As repeat offenders in church conflicts through the years, they, too, needed to be neutralized.

The proof of successful management of conflict cannot be determined over the short term. It requires a long-term evaluation. This church has thrived over the past decade or so. The new pastor called a year or so later by the congregation is still serving there. Two other key staff persons who were present during the intensity five conflict still serve the congregation with great effectiveness. The congregation continues to grow in quality and attendance.

COACHING INSIGHTS

- If you have experienced an intensity five conflict, how did you handle it? Could you correctly diagnose it, or did you become confused with multiple issues coming your way that included the complexity of emotion and hidden agendas?

- What has gone right in the way you have handled intensity five conflicts in your congregation? What has gone wrong? What would you do differently?

- If you are the pastor, a staff minister, or a program staff member, what have you learned about leading and managing conflict as you have addressed intensity five conflict situations? What are examples of how you have appropriately involved others, including outside third parties, in dealing with intensity five conflict situations?

- How would you define management of conflict at intensity five? When is it over? When is it likely to come up again? How can you tell the difference, and what might you do at the time to address this?

- Why is it impossible to ignore the aftermath of intensity five conflicts? Why is an outside third party necessary at intensity five? Have you ever waited until intensity five to bring in outside assistance? Why? Why not?

■ Are you clear on why no congregation needs intensity five conflicts? What, if any, good can come from an intensity five conflict situation?

PERSONAL REFLECTIONS

Your Reflections: What are your reflections on the material presented in this chapter?

_____

_____

_____

_____

Your Actions: What actions do you need to take about your life, ministry, and/or congregation based on the material presented in this chapter?

_____

_____

_____

_____

Your Accountability: How and by whom do you want to be held accountable for taking these actions?

_____

_____

_____

_____

7

The Sixth Intensity of Conflict

Discrediting Our Enemies

EXECUTIVE SUMMARY

The purpose of this chapter is to dialogue about the sixth intensity of conflict, in which leaving is not sufficient, but rather those who have left must be pursued and discredited because they are perceived as not having spiritual integrity. The question is really one of: "Whose integrity is actually at stake?" The focus will be on engaging the dysfunction in people who feel the need to carry conflict on past the incredible pain of dividing the Medes from the Persians discussed in the previous chapter. This unhealthy intensity of conflict is a lose-lose situation for everyone involved.

Image of Intensity Six

Intensity six conflict is represented by flooding that occurs so significantly that homes and other community buildings are damaged or destroyed on the west side of the river. Little or no flood damage had occurred on the east side of the river until this time. They were prepared for significant flooding, but this ended up being a true 100-year flood. So, homes and community buildings on the east side were also flooded. Everyone in the community experiences loss. Disaster relief crews must be brought in. Law enforcement officials are brought in to stop looting.

Overview of Intensity Six

No congregation deserves intensity six conflict situations. Intensity six conflict situations involve the pursuit of people beyond the former congregation and focuses on their integrity. Termination of pastors and staff ministers is not enough. Groups leaving and forming another congregation or dispersing to various congregations is not enough.

Leaders who remain in the former congregation feel the need to continue to criticize those who have left. They must discredit their enemies. They may actually pursue them to their new places of service or worship. For example, attempts may be made to keep a pastor from ever getting a new place of ministry service by questioning the pastor's spiritual and leadership integrity. Suggestions might even be made that ordination credentials need to be withdrawn from the pastor.

Laypersons who join another congregation in the area may have their integrity questioned in the community. They may be labeled as troublemakers, church hoppers who are always seeking to take control, or as ineligible to ever serve in congregational leadership positions.

When people who leave a congregation form a new congregation, attempts may be made to discredit the validity of the new congregation. The former congregation may seek to stop or taint contact by the denomination with the new congregation. They may oppose the recognition of the new congregation by the denomination. They certainly will oppose any financial assistance to the new congregation.

This is different than in intensity five conflict situations. In intensity five, if a pastor or staff minister leaves the former congregation, the majority of people feel that is enough. No reason exists to pursue the situation beyond an intensity five conflict. If lay individuals, families, or groups leave the former congregation, typically no reason exists to pursue them to their next place of worship. The fact that a termination or separation occurred is enough at intensity five. This is not enough at intensity six. Pursuit of the enemies becomes the focus. The terminated minister is seen as one who should never have another congregational leadership role. The laypersons who separated are seen as anti-Christian, and could never form a Christian congregation that others ought to affirm.

Fortunately, intensity six conflict situations do not occur often. The pain and stress of intensity five conflict is so severe that even if motivated to do so, very few people have the will to carry it to intensity six. Those that do move forward with the conflict have one or two common characteristics. First, they have spiritual and emotional issues going on in their lives that cause them to lose perspective. They are dysfunctional in their behavior. They choose not to stop fighting, and determine to carry the fight forward. Second, something really *is* wrong with one or more people who have left. They are a danger to themselves and others. The conflict management system used in the former congregation was unable to deal with these individual problems, and one or more people from the former congregation feel they must pursue the issue or issues.

In intensity six conflict situations it is possible that attorneys might get involved. This involvement is more than one side or the other seeking legal counsel to be sure they act appropriately. No, that would be more like intensity five conflict. When attorneys are involved at intensity six, it is for taking some type of legal action against whoever is perceived to be the enemy. Lawsuits are threatened. A few are actually filed in a court. More likely, some type of restitution or satisfaction is being sought that results in a financial settlement. This settlement can involve full payment of expected compensation.

If one side or the other is afraid of a possible escalation of the conflict to intensity seven, a restraining order might be sought. This is particularly true if physical harm has been threaten or is feared. In extreme situations it is even possible that arrests will be sought as criminal charges are leveled at one side or the other.

At intensity six, conversation about the conflict is very agitated. People often speak not so much about their individual anger, but about the righteous anger of the group or cause. Participants at times act as if they are part of a patriotic cause, or are fighting for universal spiritual principles. Participants in the conflict often find it difficult to stop fighting. Whereas at intensity five they could make a conscious decision to stop fighting, at intensity six that does not seem possible.

If people are still praying at intensity six, it is often not genuine prayer, but a crying out to God, such as, "Lord, I am pursuing those sinners who sought to destroy your church. We must not let them hurt your church or its people again. I promise you we will be successful at discrediting them."

Examples of the types of causes that rise to an intensity six conflict situation include, but are not limited to the following:

1. Personal vendetta between persons who may have known one another for many years both inside the congregation and inside the community. Often these vendettas begin in the community, or in inter-family relationships and are played out in the congregation.

2. Any attempt to withdraw the ordination credentials of a minister is probably an intensity six conflict. It appeals to the hierarchy and legislative functions of the relevant denomination. It probably comes about as a secondary conflict and is not the root conflict. It may actually be masking the root conflict.

3. Accusations of biblical or ecclesiastical heresy are intensity six conflict situations. These seek to end not only the relationship of a person to the local congregation, but to the denomination as well. Psychologically, people feel this is also attacking their eternity.

4. Immorality or legal difficulties that become supported by public facts or facts on record and available to the congregation can lead to intensity six conflict. Such difficulties can result from admission of guilt by one or more persons.

5. Actions individuals, groups, or congregations take that affirm a moral or ethical position not commonly held by others can create an intensity six conflict. Performing the marriage of persons of the same gender, or breaking the law in acts of civil disobedience such as declaring a church facility as a sanctuary for illegal immigrants, are examples of this. In many churches ordaining a woman who is then called as the senior pastor of the congregation can lead to intensity six conflict.

6. The existence in the congregation of people whose anger is so intense that it gives evidence of a psychological disorder can lead to intensity six conflict. When these people have become endorsed as leaders—even informal ones—they are able to rally many supporters who may not share their intensity, but follow their lead.

7. Property issues when a congregation seeks to separate from its denomination that holds title to the property, or at least a lien on the property, can result in intensity six conflict.

Congregational Illustrations of Intensity Six

Staff and Worship Conflict in Good Shepherd Church

The music director has moved outside of his home conference. He desires to get involved in local church ministry in his new location. Because of pressure from the leaders from his former conference, he is unable to get standing in the new conference. He chooses to accept a position with a new nondenominational congregation with a contemporary praise worship format. The former pastor of the congregation does not have an easy time at his new congregation. Some members of his former congregation, who had already left his previous congregation before he was reappointed, oppose his appointment to the new congregation. The bishop stands by his appointment, but the pastor is only able to stay at this congregation for two rocky years. Even then, people from this new congregation raise issues about the pastor's ordination status and pursue this for a year or two before finally giving up their effort.

Some of the lay leaders from the former congregation opposed the reelection of the bishop at the end of her current term, feeling that the bishop had failed their congregation. However, the bishop is successfully reelected.

Leadership vs. Management in Trinity Church

Intensity six conflict develops when the pastor of the remaining congregation approaches the pastor of the congregation where many of the fourteen people transferred their membership. He wants to make sure the pastor of their new congregation understands the problems his congregation has accepted in taking these persons into their membership. The pastor of the new congregation had no idea of the apparent gravity of the situation, and is very appreciative.

This congregation in which the people from the congregation in conflict have connected does not have a congregational style of decision-making. It actually has an elder rule. As such, it is able to successfully keep any of these people from getting into any influential roles in the life of the congregation. At first this is fine because the people are wounded by the situation at their former congregation. Eventually this is no longer fine, as they begin to express the desire to be asked to serve in leadership positions. But they are shut out from these leadership roles.

Women's Bible Study Group in Grace Church

Intensity six conflict occurs when either the pastor was terminated, or the congregation split at intensity five. If the pastor was terminated, at intensity six conflict some of the leaders of the congregation from which he was terminated are trying to pressure denominational officials to withdraw his ordination credentials because they do not think he has the spiritual integrity to be pastor of a congregation. A routine annual audit of the congregation's finances has also raised questions about his use of the congregation's credit card during the last two months he was pastor.

If the congregation splits, the congregation from which the new congregation separates seeks to put pressure on denominational officials not to provide financial support for this new congregation, nor do anything else that would recognize and give legitimacy to the new congregation. In this case, the pastor went out with the new congregation and needs the official recognition of the denomination to be able to continue participation in the insurance and pension programs in which he is enrolled.

Addressing Intensity Six Conflict

"Getting to *Neutral!*" is the theme of intensity six conflict. The congregation and its leadership are already damaged. You cannot undo the damage you and others may have caused. Those still in the congregation and those who have left will have to discover new ways of relating to God, one another, and the context they serve.

All who were involved in the conflict must find a way to have a new beginning. They must get to a neutral place from which they can build a new spiritual movement that may bring hope and peace. It is not possible to do this by simply ignoring the patterns of the past. It must begin by accepting the patterns of the past, seeing what you can learn from them, and then building a new foundation from which to move forward.

This is difficult to do if the conflict is still going on. If you are being pursued or doing the pursuing, you cannot get to neutral. One goal should be to protect yourself. If you are being pursued beyond reason, you must find ways to protect your integrity and standing in your denominational or faith-based network. If you are the pursuer and have claim to a legitimate intensity six conflict that must be engaged, then you must be careful to deal with issues that are legitimate and can be proven. Otherwise, you are doing violence and expose yourself to legal action.

Outside assistance is mandatory. All parties still involved in conflict must have third parties around them who can help them gain perspective about the emotions they are feeling and how they are expressing them. In addition, a third party must be involved in managing the relationship between the various parties still engaging in conflictual actions.

Too often, at intensity six, the third parties involved are attorneys. Arbitration would be a role that is pseudo-legal, but short of a client represented by an attorney facing a client represented by an attorney. In these situations the greatest winners are usually the attorneys.

The people who are part of the congregation from which people were terminated, and out of which groups separated, are generally having the greatest difficulty at intensity six. The people who left are often doing much better. The people who stayed may still be in a toxic environment. They may be dysfunctional. The people who left have escaped that environment for the most part. They may be moving toward a new, even stronger, functionality.

The fact that the people who leave are doing better is one thing that motivates the people who stay to continue to pursue them. Those who stay feel they must discredit those who leave. They are consumed by their own anger. Winning did not satisfy them. Termination did not satisfy them. Separation of laypersons from the congregation did not satisfy them.

Only the use of legal force or authority can keep the groups from fighting. Separation of the groups will help, but this separation must be enforced, or the fighting will renew.

Health

Health is a critical issue in intensity six conflict situations. All the people involved are subject to multiple health difficulties due to the stress level they are carrying. The existence of unhealthy levels of stress does not start at intensity five. It actually starts for many people at intensity four.

At intensity six, however, the stress load carried by people on various sides of the conflict has now been going on long enough, at a deep enough intensity, that it is impacting their health in ways that may be permanent. Various areas of a person's health may be impacted. Let's focus on three—spiritual health, physical health, and emotional or psychological health.

Spiritual Health

Intensity six conflict situations can separate you from God. Even if you are "right" or justified in your feelings or actions, the possibility exists that you will now be less than loving and gracious at any given time. When this becomes your pattern, it begins to separate you from God.

Following an unhealthy intensity of conflict, personal renewal is an essential part of healing and reconciliation. It is especially important by the time you are involved in intensity six.

Physical Health

Stress intense enough to become distress contributes to and aggravates existing physical ailments that typically are handled in mild ways. There may even be physical conditions of which we are not aware that come to our attention in the midst of conflict situations.

By intensity six, everyone who is an active participant in conflict needs to be seeking a medical evaluation to be sure that physical conditions are not contributing to their involvement in the conflict and are not being aggravated by the conflict.

Emotional or Psychological Health

By intensity six, many participating persons are carrying more stress than they can easily handle. Participants need to be aware of this. Participants need to engage in stress-reducing activities if they are going to be helpful and constructive participants in the conflict.

People who do not find ways to address the stress they are experiencing will often continue to be, or become, unhelpful people in the conflict situation. Unable to see the whole picture or system, they will speak and act out of emotion that is totally subjective. They will experience and give evidence of psychological disorders.

Some Wild Cards

Several "wild cards" need to be mentioned regarding intensity six conflict situations. First, what if the healthy people are able to stay in the congregation and the unhealthy people leave? Then much of the dialogue in this chapter simply needs to be reversed. The key principle is the aggressors versus those who are the object of aggression.

Second, what if both sides are aggressors? It does happen. One side, however, is generally willing to carry the conflict to one intensity greater than is the other side. What comes into play here is the wise judgment of Solomon in discerning the mother of a child both mothers claimed. The side that is the greatest aggressor will be willing for the greatest harm to take place. The side that is the least aggressor will want to discover ways to salvage a Christlike relationship.

Third, what if the people who leave—pastor, staff minister, or lay individuals or groups—really are dysfunctional and have active or passive tendencies that may cause harm to themselves and others. Should they be pursued? That is a strong judgment call requiring a lot of personal discernment and affirmation from others on the outside who can also see the situation. Yes, in this case these people probably should be pursued, but not directly by the people with whom they have been in conflict in the congregation.

If you feel individuals or groups are harmful or potentially harmful to others, it is your responsibility to bring this to the attention of people who can and ought to address the situation, and then you should back away. You may not ultimately be able to handle these situations.

COACHING BREAK

✔ Gaze out the window for a minute. Ponder the situation of your congregation. What images come to mind?

✔ What, if any, are examples of intensity six conflicts that you have experienced in the life and ministry of your congregation? How did your congregation handle these issues? How were you able to deal with the destruction of relationships that were a part of this situation?

✔ When you think back to your previous experiences with intensity six issues, if any, were you able to focus on "Getting to *Neutral!*," or did the destruction continue? How would you address some of these issues differently knowing that intensity six has permanent health consequences for all involved?

✔ What type of ground rules do you think need to govern an intensity six conflict situation? What ground rules would be most helpful and empowering of a solution? What ground rules would actually be harmful and controlling and continue the destruction?

What Can Go Right at Intensity Six?

1. It is difficult to think about anything positive coming out of intensity six conflict situations, short of the direct, dramatic, and divine intervention of God.

2. The intervention of legal authorities and other professionals who understand the dynamics of these situations may be able to stop the insanity of continual pursuit or to deal directly with a real problem that must be handled.
3. The new congregation or ministry placement experienced by the people who leave can be a place of great worship, love, and mission.
4. The congregation or ministers who stay can be confronted with their dysfunctional behavior by people with authority who can force them to look at the conflict situation in different ways. Without the compelling force of an outside authority, this may not happen in many congregations.
5. Manipulation and actions to organize secondary conflicts are recognized and stopped. The remaining congregation, with the assistance of an outside authority, says to its strongest antagonists that enough is enough.
6. Legal agreements or settlements are reached between those who continue to fight with one another. If not, these persons who continue to be antagonists are themselves discredited, their integrity successfully questioned, and they are separated from the remaining or emerging congregation.
7. Antagonistic leaders are replaced with people who are ready to move forward to build a new sense of Christian community in the remaining or new congregation. Health issues of all who are willing are addressed holistically as part of the new ministry of the congregation.

What Can Go Wrong at Intensity Six?

1. Nothing positive comes out of the situation. Both the remaining congregation and the new congregation become dysfunctional and keep trying to fight with one another. Ministers who remain or are separated vilify their opponents and seek to discredit them.
2. The intervention of legal authorities or other professionals fails to manage the situation. One or more people, or one of the sides in the original conflict, seem to have an "Armageddon" mentality about the situation, and no one is sure what is going to happen next.
3. Both the remaining congregation and the new congregation are unable to establish a new sense of spiritual community. Although they function regularly like congregations, it is hard to see that genuine worship, discipleship, fellowship, and mission are occurring in them.

4. The dysfunctional behavior of people who remain in the congregation continues. Although settlements of various types may be reached and outwardly the congregation seems to be doing fine, it is simply waiting for the next issues that will ignite a new round of unhealthy conflict.
5. The fighting inside the congregation has not ceased. Other staff folks are terminated. Other lay families or groups are made to feel unwelcome. The coalition that brought the previous conflict to a head now divides and fights one another.
6. Legal agreements or settlements are not reached. If the courts get involved, they may refuse to rule on what they consider an internal church issue.
7. Antagonistic leaders are able to continue to control the remaining congregation. They build a deep culture of hate rather than love that immobilizes the congregation. The long-term future of the congregation becomes one of repeated dysfunctional activities and an ongoing dysfunctional culture. Short pastorates become a pattern as no one can please these antagonistic leaders. The congregation is labeled as a toxic church.

No Congregation Deserves Intensity Six Conflict Situations

The good news is that only a small percent of congregations will ever experience this intensity of conflict. However, the few that do will more than likely be repeat offenders unless some spiritual, ecclesiastical, or grassroots movement within the congregation alters its course.

Congregations who repeatedly experience intensity six conflict become cultural enclaves rather than Christ-centered, faith-based communities. The new congregation that separates out in intensity five does not deserve the dysfunction of the former congregation that emerges at intensity six. The ministers who are terminated do not deserve the reputation of having been connected with a toxic congregation following them their entire remaining ministry.

While every congregation needs a little conflict, no congregation needs intensity six conflict.

A Congregation Unable to Handle Intensity Six Conflict

No congregation can adequately handle an intensity six conflict without harm to everyone involved. Such was the case with First Church of Murphy. Before they sought to engage a conflict management consultant, they had already terminated their pastor.

The substantive issues of conflict did not appear to be serious. What were serious were the attitudes and emotional immaturity of various members who could not stop fighting. Now that the pastor was gone, they wanted two other staff persons gone, and all who supported them. They ultimately got their wish.

It was also a time of controversy within the denominational family of this congregation. The internal split in the congregation was roughly along the political lines that had been drawn in the national conflict of their denomination. It was also a tenure fight between the people who had been around for thirty years or more, and those who had not. A godfather-like figure in the church was a retired high school football coach. Many leaders of the congregation had played football for him and wanted the congregation to go back to what it was like during their high school and young adult years.

The consultant was unable to get the various factions to agree to talk to one another. There was a question as to whether or not to complete the consultation process. The facts did not support the position of those who wanted to keep fighting; the emotion did; the power of these people did. The consultant was threatened that if his report did not call for the termination of at least two specific staff people that the lay leadership would handle that within thirty days.

The consultant could not in good conscience recommend their termination. A week after his report, the congregation split into two congregations. More than 150 people left the congregation along with the two staff persons and formed a new congregation. They thrived. They are still thriving.

The remaining congregation who "won" the battle has suffered for many years, always finding other things about which to fight. Their dysfunction has continued unhealthy patterns for the congregation and many members.

COACHING INSIGHTS

■ Before reading this chapter, how did you handle an intensity six conflict (if you've ever had one)? Could you correctly diagnose it? Probably so. It is easier to see because of the public nature of this intensity. Everyone knows about "that" church.

■ If you have ever had to deal with an intensity six conflict in your congregation, what went right, if anything, in the way you handled it? What went wrong? What would you do differently?

■ If you are the pastor, a staff minister, or a program staff member, what have you learned about leading and managing conflict as you have addressed intensity six conflict situations? What are examples of how you have appropriately involved others in dealing with intensity six conflict situations? Is it possible you have been able to avoid these toxic congregations completely?

■ How would you define management of conflict at intensity six? When is it over? When is it likely to come up again? How can you tell the difference, and what might you do at the time to address this?

■ What reasons do you believe support the premise that no congregation deserves intensity six conflict situations? What can be learned from these situations that may empower the future life and ministry of your congregation? How can you share these learnings throughout your congregation and thus increase your capacity to handle conflict situations?

PERSONAL REFLECTIONS

Your Reflections: What are your reflections on the material presented in this chapter?

_____

_____

_____

_____

_____

Your Actions: What actions do you need to take about your life, ministry, and/or congregation based on the material presented in this chapter?

_____

_____

_____

_____

_____

Your Accountability: How and by whom do you want to be held accountable for taking these actions?

_____

_____

_____

_____

_____

8

The Seventh Intensity of Conflict

Destroying the Infidels

EXECUTIVE SUMMARY

The purpose of this chapter is to dialogue about the seventh intensity of conflict, in which dysfunctional persons actually seek to physically harm participants in a congregation, or seek to destroy the congregational facilities. The focus will be on understanding that a few situations, aggravated by unhealthy personalities, can get to a point of a vendetta by one person or cause against another person, group, or the entire congregation. Thankfully, these situations are few and far between in comparison to the typical existence of conflict in congregations. Nothing but losses can exist in a situation in which lives and property are not only threatened with harm, but people also act on their threats.

Image of Intensity Seven

Intensity seven conflict is represented by flooding that occurs so severely and quickly that not only were homes and community buildings were destroyed, but people on the west side of the river became trapped in various building with no escape routes. Numerous deaths occurred. The people on the east side thought they were protected from harm, but they experienced three deaths when a mother and her two preschool children were swept away by the current of the raging river that jumped its river bed and formed a new path. The communities struggled with the deaths and what, if anything, they could have done to prevent them.

Overview of Intensity Seven

No congregation deserves intensity seven conflict.

Intensity seven conflicts exist when the focus is on doing intentional harm to people or to congregational facilities. It is an extremely unhealthy situation that is lose-lose for everyone involved. Participants in the conflict are treating it as an "Armageddon" situation. They feel it is better for all to be hurt than for the current situation to be allowed to continue. Hurt experienced in the extreme is death.

Few congregational conflict situations ever escalate to this intensity of conflict. It could even be argued this intensity does not need to be included in the system. My response is that because these situations do occasionally happen, we need to address this intensity.

Emotions are totally out of control on at least one side of the conflict, and perhaps on both sides. People who would involve themselves as antagonists in intensity seven conflict situations are emotionally and psychologically out of control. In short, they are sick. But sick people can take real actions just as well as they can fantasize about them.

Intensity seven conflicts go beyond the legal actions involving lawsuits or involving criminal accusations. They go beyond ecclesiastical actions of defrocking or church discipline. They are now at the stage of warlike actions.

Individuals, groups, or organizations intentionally choose to engage in actions that harm people and destroy property. Their tools are no longer words, documents, arguments, or formal compelling actions characteristic of board or organizational votes. Their tools are fists, knives, guns, poisons, fire, and other such destructive tools. Perhaps you can see why I would say these people are sick.

Actions that appear to represent anarchy may occur at this intensity. The conflicts are violent. In large groups or governments these conflicts become military actions or war. The object is to harm the other. If this harm results in death, that is seen as necessary for truth to prevail.

The opposition does not just need to be out of sight, as in the case in intensity five conflict situations. The opposition, in the case of pastors and church staff ministers, does not simply need to be discredited so they will never minister again as in intensity six conflict. The opposition needs to be gone forever so there is no chance they will ever come back. They need to be maimed or killed.

If a separation group has formed a new congregation, it does not just need to be discredited; someone needs to stop it from meeting and functioning as a congregation. To accomplish this, people in the new congregation need to be hurt, or the congregational meeting place destroyed. In the development of such a situation, as this conflict passed through intensity six, antagonists tried to get legal and ecclesiastical authorities to handle the situation. They did not. Now the antagonists become vigilantes who will take care of it individually or as a group.

If a separation group is still feeling antagonism toward the congregation that excluded them, they may try similar actions against that congregation. Pastors and other staff who are terminated, as well as pastors and staff who terminate others, may feel their enemies need to be destroyed and may act on their feelings directly or manipulate someone else to do so.

Are you glad yet that this conflict intensity happens very seldom?

In their emotional and spiritual sickness at intensity seven, some antagonists actually feel they are special agents from God carrying out a cleansing. They may even pray, "Lord, as your special agent, I am eliminating the infidels! Thank you for using me in your service."

Language at intensity seven is very hostile and highly explosive. The participants reflect an attitude that they are now part of an eternal cause. Because they are sick, they cannot stop fighting. The cost to the church and God of withdrawal from the fight is perceived as greater than the cost of continuing the fight. Therefore, only outside authority will be able to stop antagonists at intensity seven.

A surprise at intensity seven is that people, who under other circumstances might not express anger that is out of control, will do so when one or more particular issues drive them to this intensity. They snap. They may even for a while feel justified. They do not believe government law or God's law override the feelings they have to do harm.

The harm people choose to do is not always confined to the people with whom they are the angriest. At times it is also focused on themselves. So, just as they will seek to harm—even kill—others, they may seek to do harm to themselves. Suicide is not uncommon.

Examples of the types of causes that rise to an intensity seven conflict situation include, but are not limited to the following:

1. Retribution for harm one person or group feels another person or group has done to them. The harm that is felt to have taken place does not have to have involved violence and physical harm. It could have been actions characteristic of intensity five or six. However, the rage it creates in some people to get retribution will raise the intensity of the conflict.
2. Public embarrassment and discrediting of an individual or group by another individual or group can, in a very few cases, cause another escalation of the conflict, and the individual or group embarrassed or discredited can carry out a vendetta against those seen as antagonists.
3. A response to severe immoral activity by an individual or group can result in intensity seven actions.
4. If a person, and this is in the category of when religion gets sick, believes the actions of another has damaged the possibility for attaining eternal life with God, that person may strike out at those considered to be his or her antagonist.
5. If a person feels his or her ability to get a job in his or her chosen field has been harmed by an individual or group, then he or she may lash out at those seen as antagonists.
6. Continuing to fight with people who have a psychological disorder can result in intensity seven actions.
7. When an individual or group feels others have stolen something from them and the only way to get it back is by violent action. In extreme cases this may be the chosen path.

Congregational Illustrations of Intensity Seven

Staff and Worship Conflict in Good Shepherd Church

The stress of multiple years of conflict began to take a toll on the pastor. Various health issues began to plague him. Following the two rocky years at a new congregational appointment, he was forced to take early retirement at age sixty due to the fragile nature of his health. He was now only able to function as a chaplain in the local senior adult long-term care facility.

The music director actually soared in his ministry. The nondenominational congregation became a regional model of a positive contemporary congregation, excellent quality praise and worship, and in-depth disciple-making processes. He married a woman in the new contemporary congregation whose husband had died in Iraq. Together they had a son who became a blessing to both of them. This was particularly important as his former wife stabilized her life, went to court, and was successful in gaining primary custody of her daughters.

Good Shepherd never recovered. In a way it was too late. By the time they had the intervention of a conflict management consultant, they had already hardwired into their congregational culture the destructive behavior of being a repeat offender of conflict. Each year they were weaker and older. Within a decade they existed only at subsistence level, without vital ministry. They had shot themselves in the foot years before and were dying of complications.

Leadership vs. Management in Trinity Church

Intensity seven conflict raises its head when the former chairperson of the finance committee at Trinity Church makes an appointment to see his former pastor. His intentions were to try to apologize and reconcile. The first part of the conversation does not go well. Old wounds open up. Both the layperson and the pastor begin saying things that are inappropriate and unloving. Ultimately, they shout at one another. The church staff, hearing the shouting, wonders if they should intervene.

Hearing the pastor scream, they rush into the office to find the former finance committee chairperson grabbing his chest and falling on the floor. They rush over to help him, but immediately cannot find a pulse. He has died of a massive heart attack.

The next day, the pastor asks for a leave of absence to get away for a while. Five months later, he resigns as pastor and leaves the active ordained ministry, never to return again.

Women's Bible Study Group in Grace Church

Intensity seven conflict becomes real during a chance encounter between the former pastor and a person from the old congregation in which the conflict started, who is perceived to be a dysfunctional individual. Enraged by the circumstances of the split, how badly the old congregation is now doing, and blinded by his own rage, he takes a swing at the former pastor, decks him on the sidewalk, and kicks the door panel of the pastor's car, denting it.

Intensity seven is also expressed through the teenagers from the old congregation in the high school that Kim's daughter attends. They taunt her, slash her tires in the school parking lot, and spread false rumors about her involvement with illegal drugs and that she is bulimic.

It is further expressed by a participant in the split congregation going into the old congregation's facilities, using a master key he did not give back when he left the congregation, and taking things he thinks belong to him. He had bought some preschool equipment with his own money, and believes he deserves to take them to the new congregation. Several items were attached to the walls, and some damage was done to the rooms from which the equipment items were taken.

Addressing Intensity Seven Conflict

"Getting to *Neutral!*" is the theme of intensity seven conflict. The participants in the conflict have been discredited. Their integrity has been wounded. All have lost something. Attempts to heal and reconcile have failed.

Conflict participants may actually be in open fear of one another. Part of this fear is of the unknown. They do not know what the other will do, when they will do it, or where they will do it. Strategies of offensive and defensive war arise. Should they engage in preemptive activities? These would involve situations in which evidence exists your opponent is getting ready to attack you, so you attack them first.

Should they engage in preventative activities? These would involve situations in which some evidence exists that at some future date your opponent might have the capacity to attack you, particularly in an area in which you would have an inadequate defense. Therefore, you attack them before their capacity to attack you is developed.

Should they engage in defensive activities? These would involve situations in which you believe you may be attacked. But you do not want to do anything until you are actually attacked. Yet you are preparing for an attack and figuring out how you can both defend yourself and launch a counterattack, if it seems warranted. The reality is that, given any reason, you will probably launch a counterattack, because your emotions are already so out of control.

None of these strategies that come out of fear will appropriately address intensity seven conflict situations. And, remember, this is a book about congregational conflict. For the vast majority of you, the likelihood of intensity seven conflict actions is slim and none.

However, if it is possible, imminent, or does occur without adequate notice, it is unlikely you can address it directly. There is nothing Christlike about countering intensity seven actions with other intensity seven actions. That is "Armageddon."

Law enforcement must be brought in to deal with intensity seven actions. Participants have to be restrained by law enforcement in the short-term, and dealt with in the legal, criminal system in the long-term, to keep them from harming others and themselves. Do not wait until it is too late to notify these appropriate third parties. Contact them armed with evidence of what is happening.

Death

Congregations die. People die. Both of these are real situations. Intensity seven conflict situations kill organizations and people. Death is final. It is permanent. The perpetrators of death often die themselves.

In the case of congregations, intensity seven conflict situations impact both the congregation that is the object of the aggression and the congregation that is the perpetrator of the aggression. Similar things can be said about individual and group participants. Often intensity seven conflict actions occur between an individual or group and another individual or group, and not necessarily in their congregation.

The death of a congregation does not always mean it ceases to exist. It can also mean it becomes a cultural enclave without any spiritual focus or action. It is simply going through the motions of being a local regular gathering of people who like to call themselves a church. Both congregations who are the objects of aggression and congregations who are the perpetrators of aggression may experience this type of death. Both lose. God is not honored. The Church is not respected. The reputation of Christian religious organizations is once again smeared.

Following death can come resurrection. Individuals, groups, and congregations can be transformed. This transformation will not occur by means of a sharp business plan or great group dynamics. It will occur because of the direct, dramatic, divine intervention of God, the true giver of life eternal. A congregation cannot demand this new life. It cannot position itself for new life. It can only receive new life from God. It can pray for it. It can humble itself to receive it. It can choose to totally give itself over to God in a spirit of repentance.

COACHING BREAK

✔ Gaze out the window for a minute. Ponder the situation of your congregation. What images come to mind?

✔ Have you ever experienced an intensity seven conflict situation? What was it like? How were people and churches harmed? What was its direct and indirect impact on you?

✔ When you think about your experience (if any) with intensity seven issues, were you able to focus on "Getting to *Neutral!*," or did you feel the need to harm or destroy the other? How would you address intensity seven situations if they occur again? What would you do to keep conflict from escalating to this intensity?

✔ What type of law enforcement and legal resources do you need to call on for intensity seven conflict situations? How would you build a case that was based on solid truth to get their attention? What would you do if you could not get their attention?

What Can Go Right at Intensity Seven?

1. It is highly unlikely anything positive would immediately come forth from an intensity seven situation. When people are hurt or killed, the word positive or the thought of something going right does not occur.
2. As a result of an intensity seven situation, individuals, groups, and congregations who see this tragedy may be shocked to the point they will change their patterns of behavior in a dramatic way that avoids these types of situations in the future.
3. The intervention of legal authorities and law enforcement may be able to stop or contain the spread of the violence exhibited in an isolated location or situation, just as firefighters would seek to stop or contain the spread of a fire.
4. Wise observers may be able to help the larger Church learn from this situation so that more loving patterns of relating could emerge.
5. Truly psychotic individuals may be stopped and their long-term psychoses addressed.

6. God may break through in a direct, dramatic, and divine manner here or at any stage in the escalating conflict situation.
7. New leaders emerge in the congregation who are able, with God's leadership, to refocus the remnant within the congregation—or the majority in some cases—to transform their approach to Christian ministry.

What Can Go Wrong at Intensity Seven?

1. Death and destruction are everywhere. Not only is it a lose-lose situation in terms of organizational dynamics, but people are really harmed and may die. Church organizations and physical facilities are damaged or destroyed. Everyone loses.
2. Too many people are desensitized to conflict of this nature and impact and are not motivated to avoid this type of tragedy in their situation, but are destined to repeat it.
3. The intervention of legal authorities and law enforcement was too little, too late. The violence spread into other lives, families, and/or congregations.
4. No one emerged or was successful in helping the larger Church learn something from this situation.
5. Psychotic individuals were actually enabled by this situation and went on to repeat these actions in other situations.
6. No new leaders emerged in the impacted congregations, and they suffered a long, painful death.

No Congregation Deserves Intensity Seven Conflict

The great news is that hardly any congregational conflict situations get to this intensity. None who experience them need them. Spiritual, ecclesiastical, or grassroots movements often intervene in these situations before intensity seven. This intervention can be formal or informal.

No individual sin or collection of sins justifies the violence of intensity seven conflict situations. No individuals deserve to be harmed or killed. While every congregation needs a little conflict, obviously no congregation needs intensity seven conflicts.

A Congregation That Died as a Result of Intensity Seven Conflict

Summit Heights flirted with death several times. Twenty years before it actually closed its doors, it flirted with death by cutting itself off from its community and trying to be a cultural enclave.

Members fought one another and their pastor until the congregation had almost no fight left. In one board meeting, the pastor stood between two leaders ready to throw punches to settle their conflict. Then the congregation rediscovered ministry in its community and thrived for a few years.

Economic hardships arose in the church ten years later. Congregants driving into its inner-city context were run off by the neighborhood people because the congregants did not understand the neighborhood and its people. The church ended up merging with another struggling inner-city congregation and bought itself some time. While the members did not throw real rocks, the verbal rocks they cast when conflicts arose were just as painful.

Adding to the toxic nature of the congregation was the next pastor following the merger, who was himself toxic. He saw the hard-working, community-ministry–focused people as the enemy, and the pew sitters as his friends. He tried to marginalize the creative and innovative people. When things got tough, the pew sitters abandoned him, while—ironically—the people of passion kept the congregation going. The pastor's car was regularly vandalized during his tenure. This was unusual because typically the pastor of this church was highly respected in the community and protected from the violence of this neighborhood.

Finally, the congregation reached a point at which they had too few people with too little passion to keep the doors open. No catastrophic violent act killed this congregation. A series of intractable situations doomed it as a Christ-centered community, and several years later as a cultural organization. It died of natural causes.

COACHING INSIGHTS

■ Before reading this chapter, how did you handle an intensity seven conflict (if you ever had one)? Could you correctly diagnose it? It would probably be obvious. Its actions are broadcast to many others, and at times to the whole world.

■ What, if any, are the right ways to handle intensity seven conflicts in your congregation? If you have ever had to deal with one, what went right? What went wrong? What would you do differently, other than to avoid these conflicts like the plague?

■ If you are the senior pastor, a staff minister, or a program staff member, what have you learned about leading and managing conflict if you have addressed intensity seven conflict situations? How might you go forward in ministry without being traumatized by fear that an intensity seven conflict might occur again some day?

■ How would you define management of conflict at intensity seven? When is it over? When is it likely to come up again? How can you tell the difference, and what might you do at the time to address this?

■ How can you avoid intensity seven conflict situations? Have you really ever known someone who engaged an intensity seven conflict who was not him- or herself a victim of that engagement? If so, how did that come about?

■ What reasons do you believe support the premise that no congregation deserves intensity seven conflict situations? What can be learned from these situations that may empower the future life and ministry of your congregation? How can you share these learnings throughout your congregation and thus increase your capacity to handle conflict situations?

PERSONAL REFLECTIONS

Your Reflections: What are your reflections on the material presented in this chapter?

_____

_____

_____

_____

_____

Your Actions: What actions do you need to take about your life, ministry, and/or congregation based on the material presented in this chapter?

_____

_____

_____

_____

Your Accountability: How and by whom do you want to be held accountable for taking these actions?

_____

_____

_____

_____

_____

9

Leadership Styles for Engaging Conflict

EXECUTIVE SUMMARY

The purpose of this chapter is to dialogue about various leadership styles available to address the different intensities of conflict. The focus will be on explaining these leadership styles and suggesting when it might be most appropriate to use these styles. In addition, general information will be shared about various third-party roles that might be helpful at various intensities of conflict.

Leadership Styles within Congregations

Various leadership styles and characteristics are expressed in the life of congregations. Some work well in conflict situations, and some do not. Some work well at one intensity of conflict, and others do not.

For many years I have relied on the instrument created by Speed Leas of The Alban Institute to identify seven conflict leadership styles that may be helpful at various intensities of conflict. Speed developed these more than twenty years ago and related them to his five levels of conflict. While I have continued to use his seven styles, I have modulated—in my understanding of the definition of these styles—when to use various styles, and how to apply them to the seven intensities of conflict.

I would encourage you to go to www.Alban.org and secure a copy of *Discover Your Conflict Management Style* (revised edition) by Speed Leas. It was published in 1997 by The Alban Institute, now in Herndon, Va. This is a useful instrument and should be taken by the leaders of your congregation to help them discover their conflict management leadership style(s). When they complete the instrument, they should do so thinking about conflict situations in the congregation in which they are participants. This is called two-party conflict perspective, meaning the person taking the instrument is associated with one of the parties, or is one of the key parties, involved in the conflict.

This is different from third-party conflict perspective, in which a person sees him- or herself as a third party who is outside the conflict looking in and seeking to provide some guidance for those involved in the conflict. A third-party perspective generates a different set of conflict management leadership styles when taking this instrument because the role in conflict situations is different.

The revised instrument has some updates to it from when I developed my concepts surrounding the conflict management leadership styles. Let me share my seven designations with you and the definitions I have been using based originally on the work of Speed Leas. The seven conflict management leadership styles are *Support, Avoid, Accommodate, Persuade, Collaborate, Negotiate,* and *Compel.*

Support

Support is a style that recognizes everyone as persons of worth created in the image of God to live and to love. As such they are worthy of spiritual, physical, emotional, and psychological support and affirmation.

Avoid

Avoid is a style that acknowledges not every conflict issue or situation has to be engaged or should be engaged. Some can or should be avoided.

Lower intensity conflicts can be avoided because some will work themselves out, some will typically be engaged by others with greater passion about them and you do not need to be involved, and some will escalate if you engage them if you are not directly involved in them.

At high intensities of conflict some should be avoided because you are likely to get hurt if you try to engage them rather than let appropriate authority figures do so. Some should be avoided because you will become a victim if you get involved inappropriately.

Accommodate

Accommodate is an appropriate style when many right answers exist. Only the most controlling people feel they must have their specific answer or solution to every situation.

Wise people affirm and support various ideas or solutions that empower grassroots people to handle healthy conflict and learn conflict management leadership skills.

Persuade

Persuade is a style to use when mild attempts to convince others that a certain solution or solutions will work appear to be a helpful and hopeful strategy. *Persuade* is popularly seen in two forms. The first form involves an individual, often an individual in leadership, seeking to persuade one or more individuals that certain solutions will work in the current situation, if they can all embrace these solutions. A second form that is a natural part of congregational culture involves a speaker, generally the senior pastor, seeking to persuade a congregation through proclamation that a certain solution or solutions should work in a given situation.

It should be acknowledged that *Persuade*, a style very characteristic of some pastoral leaders, can come across as a parent-to-child transactional approach. In these cases the leader—perhaps the senior pastor—is in the role of parent, and those being persuaded are in the role of children. At times those being persuaded may feel they are being taken advantage of, and may eventually resent or reject the actions of the leader.

Collaborate

Collaborate is an adult-to-adult transactional approach that seeks to bring equals together to work on solutions that can be empowering or synergistic. It is a group or team approach to conflict resolution and mediation. It brings together relevant people for dialogue.

If there are two identified positions or sides, let's call one blue and the other yellow. Blue and yellow dialogue with one another long enough and deeply enough that they arrive at new solutions to their challenges. The solutions are represented by the color green. The solutions then are a transformation of the two positions and involve the discovery of new ways of thinking and acting that are greater than either of the two beginning positions.

Negotiate

Negotiate is the traditional bargaining or compromise position. It seeks a solution by coming up with an acceptable position that is a compromise between two presented positions. It is a style that is typical of labor negotiations or international relationships between countries.

The blue position and the yellow position come together in the middle and form a striped position that has a little blue and a little yellow in it. The challenge is that neither side is completely satisfied nor feels they got to a long-term acceptable solution. The next time issues arise, they will want to bring up the places they did not win before and place them back on the agenda for further dialogue.

Compel

Compel involves force or coercion by formal governance processes, or by a professional conflict management process that uses formal procedures and ground rules. It can also occur negatively through bullying or attacking. It is the most forceful style, and only comes into play once the conflict is no longer in healthy intensities. It can begin with something as simple as the typical forms of voting in an organization that mandate actions according to the vote.

Each person tends to have one or two conflict management leadership styles as his or her lead or dominant styles. At times a third style may cluster at the top. Each person also tends to have one or two styles that are least characteristic of his or her leadership style.

Some leadership styles are also more active than others. The most active styles are *Compel, Negotiate, Collaborate,* and *Persuade.* The least active styles are *Avoid, Accommodate,* and *Support.* It is ideal for both the most and least active leadership styles to be present in the leadership of a congregation.

Patterns of Conflict Management Leadership Styles

The pattern of conflict management leadership styles present in each congregation is unique. However, some observations can be made and conclusions drawn from patterns that have been observed over the past twenty-five years. First, *Support, Avoid,* and

Accommodate are very popular styles possessed by congregational leaders. Because these roles are often more passive than active, they are characteristic of the general desire of congregations to avoid conflict situations and either affirm the people involved in conflict as persons of worth, or accommodate people involved in conflict because we do not want to confront them.

Second, *Persuade* is often one of the styles characteristic of the senior pastor. Much of a pastor's life and ministry is based on the practice of persuasion. Preaching is persuasion. Many leadership tasks involve persuasion. When insufficient time is available to produce collaborative solutions, then persuasion is a fall-back position.

Third, *Collaborate* is a style present in staff members and lay leaders who do a lot of work with groups, teams, and leadership communities. Many small-to medium-sized groups have decision processes that call for a collaborative style. Leaders who work this way much of the time then desire to handle conflict in a similar way.

Fourth, *Negotiate* and *Compel* are the two styles that tend to be least present in the life and ministry of a congregation. They are more complicated styles that call for advanced skill, experience, and wisdom. They are also the styles most needed when conflict is moving to a greater degree of intensity and away from healthy degrees of intensity.

Application of Leadership Styles to the Intensities of Conflict

Various conflict management leadership styles are most appropriate and needed for each of the seven intensities of conflict. (See the chart at the end of chapter 1.) At the bottom of the chart entitled *The Intensities of Congregational Conflict* is a listing of the seven leadership styles with suggestions as to when it might be appropriate to use them.

Intensity One

In intensity one conflict situations the styles of *Support, Avoid, Accommodate, Persuade,* and *Collaborate* might be appropriately used. It is always appropriate for people to receive support as persons of worth created in the image of God to live and to love. It is not always possible for this support to come from people with whom you are in conflict. But it is always appropriate to have people who support you because of your value as an individual.

It is reasonable to avoid or accommodate at intensity one. Not all conflict situations have to be engaged by everyone who is aware of them. In fact, it is not healthy to do so. Therefore, avoidance may be appropriate at intensity one. It is also not necessary to get your way, because there is no one "right" solution to resolve intensity one conflict situations. There are often many right, good, and loving answers. So, to accommodate the suggestion of someone else is often a fine thing to do.

Earlier I indicated that too often the senior pastor or other church staff gets involved in too many intensity one conflict situations. Rather than using these as an opportunity for people to learn how to make healthy decisions, these leaders rush in with a decision or answer. In dealing with an intensity one, he or she could simply nudge the process on; often this person does not need to become an active participant.

Persuade and *Collaborate* are the active leadership styles to be used at intensity one. If time is available, *Collaborate* is the preferred style. In an emergency situation or where insufficient time is available, persuasion may work as long as the overall pattern is collaboration. Always remember persuasion may not fully satisfy and may leave unfinished agendas that will arise again later.

Intensity Two

In intensity two conflict situations the same set of styles of *Support, Avoid, Accommodate, Persuade,* and *Collaborate* can be appropriately used. The dynamics have shifted, however, from issues that are task-oriented to issues that are person-oriented. The need for *Collaborate* to be the lead active style is greater. The possibility that the use of *Persuade* will create some underlying resentment that will come up again later is also greater.

Keep in mind intensities one and two conflict situations are both seen as situations that can be resolved. The use of styles and tactics that are win-lose should never be used in intensities one and two. Moving too quickly to persuasion may not necessarily resolve the issues at hand.

Intensity Three

In intensity three conflict situations the styles of *Support, Persuade, Collaborate,* and *Negotiate* can be used. Supporting people involved in a conflict situation is always appropriate, as has been mentioned. The other three styles are active styles that can be used with great promise at intensity three. Missing are *Avoid* and *Accommodate.* Why?

Intensity three conflict situations are now win-lose. Once this threshold is crossed, it is no longer appropriate to see avoidance and accommodation as positive leadership styles. They actually become unhealthy styles at this juncture. If you are a participant in a conflict, or are closely associated with participants in a conflict, then you must at least take a supportive role with individuals or a helpful process role in the conflict situation. At intensity three avoidance and accommodation become positions of denial.

Collaborate and *Persuade* continue as proactive and helpful leadership styles at intensity three. With *Persuade,* always keep in mind that some degree of permission to persuade must exist in the interaction for it to remain a healthy style.

Negotiate now appears on the scene as the new proactive style. Why has it not appeared before now? Negotiation involves compromise and bargaining. These are characteristics of win-lose situations in which not everyone, or perhaps *no one,* gets what he or she needs from the dialogue. Therefore, once negotiation is used, any situation may become a win-lose situation. The strength of negotiation is to handle situations with multiple conflict issues in which rounds of processing will be needed until there is readiness for collaboration, or obvious need for persuasion to bring closure to the dialogue.

Intensity Four

Persuade drops out as a leadership style at intensity four, and *Compel* is added for the first time. The list of preferred leadership styles is *Support, Collaborate, Negotiate,* and *Compel.* Persuasion is no longer effective at intensity four. The motives of people who seek to persuade are questioned. This phenomenon surrounding persuasion was beginning to happen at intensity three, but is in full force by intensity four.

Collaboration may still work in some intensity four situations, particularly soon after the situation moves into intensity four. However, the open, adult-to-adult dialogue that needs to occur for collaboration to work diminishes very quickly in intensity four. Collaboration works when participants never intended for the conflict to become congregation-wide and are trying to find a way to lessen the intensity before the situation gets out of hand. Therefore, to attempt collaboration early in an intensity four situation may bring success.

Negotiate and *Compel* are the leadership styles that most tend to work in intensity four situations. They are generally being carried out by an outside mediator. At this intensity it is definitely a win-lose situation, and often has the capacity to quickly move to intensity five if the situation is not adequately engaged. Negotiation is helpful to discover and implement small wins that can become big wins if there are enough of them. Compelling is a necessary and typical part of intensity four as people in the congregation begin to vote in various ways. The science and art of formal decision-making that has the power to change behaviors is needed to compel people to manage their conflicts.

Intensity Five

At intensity five, *Collaborate* is no longer a helpful style. It does not provide enough force. Participants are can no longer see dialogue and discussion as helpful. They want debate and decision. Each side believes they are right and that God is on their side. To collaborate is viewed as surrendering to the opposition.

Support is still present in its appropriate role. The leading active styles are *Negotiate* and *Compel*. They must be facilitated by an outside manager of the conflict. The congregation definitely cannot handle these situations well without outside assistance. At times the negotiation must involve the separation of people or groups from one another. Negotiation can also be used to test whether participants really intended for the situation to get out of hand and move to the incredible pain of intensity five, or if they want to find a way to de-escalate. Compelling is generally done by the governing board of the congregation, or the congregation as a whole when the polity calls for it.

Intensities Six and Seven

The leadership styles for these remaining intensities are the same. *Support* for the people involved is appropriate and really mandatory. *Negotiate* and *Compel* are the lead styles. They are fully being carried out by outside third parties if anything that will be healthy long-term is to result. If people in the conflict are trying to lead negotiations or are compelling, it is generally counterproductive and is more like bullying and attacking.

COACHING BREAK

✔ Gaze out the window for a minute. Ponder the situation of your congregation. What images come to mind?

✔ What are the conflict management leadership styles represented by the leaders of your congregation? What is your personal leadership style? How have leadership styles been expressed in conflict situations in your congregation? To what extent have the appropriate styles been expressed during the appropriate intensity?

✔ What types of things do you need to do to develop conflict management leadership style capacities within your congregation? What type of training do you need? What type of experimentation and experience do you need?

✔ What steps are needed to develop the active leadership styles of *Persuade, Collaborate, Negotiate,* and *Compel*? In addition to developing these capacities, what practice of dealing with conflict needs to be improved? What are the first steps you need to take to work on capacities and to improve your practices?

✔ To what extent are *Avoid* and *Accommodate* appropriately expressed in your congregational conflict situations? To what extent is *Support* being appropriately expressed in your congregation?

Leadership Approaches for Engaging Conflict

On the chart, *The Intensities of Congregational Conflict,* are listed some suggested leadership approaches that might involve third parties with individuals, groups, and the congregation at various intensities of conflict. (See the chart at the end of chapter 1.)

The third-party roles mentioned are *Chaplain, Personal Coach, Team Coach, Mediator, Organizational Coach, Consultant, Arbitrator, Attorney,* and *Law Enforcement*. Here is an explanation of the intended functions of each of these roles.

Chaplain

The role of *Chaplain* implies that at intensities one and two many people have formal or informal relationships with friends, ministers, or counselors who function in a *Chaplain* role to help people maintain perspective in their lives, and deal with any pinch points of assurance and relationships.

Certainly the role of *Chaplain* from someone outside the congregation, similar to the role of *Support* from someone inside the congregation, may be active throughout the conflict intensities. But what is being implied here is that it is only a proactive strategy at intensities one and two.

Personal Coach

Personal Coach suggests a formal relationship with someone who functions as a personal ministry coach. Typically this would be someone with training, certification, and experience who provides formal coaching services for individuals. This role can be the most helpful at intensities one and two when individuals and specific issues are being addressed.

Team Coach

A *Team Coach* is someone who has additional training and experience in working with groups or teams. A *Team Coach's* expertise and experience are needed particularly at intensity three for informal or formal groups or teams in the congregation who are involved in the conflict. *Collaborate* is the preferred style of dealing with the issues of conflict.

Mediator

If the issues are being expressed more in a win-lose manner, then a *Mediator* is needed to focus the dialogue around issues that can be negotiated. It is at intensity three when, for the first time, the formal engagement of an outside third party may be an appropriate step. A *Mediator* role may also work for a while in intensity four situations.

Organizational Coach

An *Organizational Coach* is needed by intensity four. This is a person with a coach approach who understands dynamics of organizations and how to work with the congregation as a whole, and at the same time work with specific leadership communities within the congregation to mediate the conflict situation. Both mediators and organizational coaches work when negotiation is the primary tactic during intensity four.

Consultant

Fairly soon during intensity four, the role of *Consultant* may need to emerge. This is necessary when compelling becomes necessary.

Consulting will involve a contract or covenant relationship, ground rules for dealing with the conflict, and checkpoints of accountability along the way. The consulting role will be an appropriate role and function at both intensities four and five.

Arbitrator

Once the conflict intensity is fully unhealthy, and terminations and separations are taking place, the role of *Arbitrator* may be necessary. This person works with the various participants as individuals or groups to develop managed solutions to the conflict. The role of an *Arbitrator* implies participants agree to abide by the recommendations of this outside third party. At times the congregational board or the full congregation may also have to vote on the recommendations. But no individual participant or groups can veto the work of the *Arbitrator*. This role is needed at intensities five and six.

Attorneys

Using *Attorneys* should be avoided as long as possible. Perhaps an attorney could be used at intensity four to moderate a business conference of the congregation or the board. Perhaps an attorney could be used at intensity five to craft severance agreements. Otherwise, their involvement should be avoided until intensity six conflict situations. Whenever an attorney is introduced into the process, this has the potential to create a situation of dueling attorneys. An attorney's involvement almost always escalates the conflict. At intensity six, however, the involvement of attorneys, and at times courts and judges, is essential to keep the situation from exploding to intensity seven.

Law Enforcement

Unfortunately, at intensity seven only *Law Enforcement* officers can handle the conflict. That is sad, but true. People are seeking to harm one another, and it takes a compelling force that is unstoppable to handle conflict that seems equally unstoppable.

Integration of Roles

These nine roles and functions that may be needed throughout the life and ministry of congregations, as they deal with various intensities of conflict, are not mutually exclusive roles and functions. Some outside third parties can function in multiple roles. For example, a *Personal Coach* may be able to function as a *Team Coach* and as an *Organizational Coach*. It depends on the person's training and experience. The biggest challenge is that if a person begins as a *Personal Coach*, he or she may be too identified with the person being coached to move to coaching teams and the congregation as a whole. Both the coach and the congregation need to be sensitive to this.

A *Mediator* can also be an *Organizational Coach*, or at times a *Consultant*. This person simply have to be clear with him- or herself and the congregation as to which role this person is playing. A *Consultant* can also function in the role of an *Arbitrator* if a contract or covenant is developed that defines this role. Roles that do not lend themselves to matching with others are *Chaplain, Attorney,* and *Law Enforcement.*

COACHING INSIGHTS

■ Before reading this chapter, how would you have viewed the conflict management leadership styles needed to engage various intensities of conflict? What leadership styles have you used in the past? Which ones have been most effective, and how was that effectiveness manifested?

■ Conflict can be embarrassing to many people. As a result, it is often true that people and congregations do not ask for outside assistance until their conflict is at an unhealthy intensity. To what extent is that true for you and your congregation? What are your criteria for asking for outside assistance to help you to positively engage your conflict situation?

■ If you are the pastor, a staff minister, or a program staff member, what have you learned about leading and managing conflict from this dialogue about leadership styles in the congregation and leadership approaches for engaging conflict? What steps do you need to take to more positively engage your own leadership style?

■ What do you need to do to have a positive feeling about calling in an outside third party to engage the conflict in your congregation? How could you start by using an outside third party to help you deal with your own perspective, skill, and emotion concerning conflict? Where would you go to find a coach who could assist you with this?

■ What reasons surrounding conflict management leadership styles do you believe support the premise that every congregation needs a little conflict? What can be learned from these leadership styles that may empower the future life and ministry of your congregation? How can you share these learnings throughout your congregation and thus increase your capacity to handle conflict situations?

PERSONAL REFLECTIONS

Your Reflections: What are your reflections on the material presented in this chapter?

_____

_____

_____

_____

Your Actions: What actions do you need to take about your life, ministry, and/or congregation based on the material presented in this chapter?

_____

_____

_____

_____

Your Accountability: How and by whom do you want to be held accountable for taking these actions?

_____

_____

_____

_____

10

Processes for Engaging Conflict

EXECUTIVE SUMMARY

The purpose of this chapter is to dialogue about processes for engaging conflict at various intensities, with a focus on *Conflict Resolution, Conflict Mediation,* and *Conflict Management.* A process for identifying the best people in your congregation to engage issues of conflict will be shared.

Processes for Engaging the Intensities of Conflict

Various processes exist for engaging the intensities of conflict. Books and other resources abound that suggest effective processes. Biblical models are also available. This chapter seeks to suggest some processes that are implied on the chart, *The Intensities of Congregational Conflict.* (See the chart at the end of chapter 1.)

Three broad approaches can be suggested—*Conflict Resolution, Conflict Mediation,* and *Conflict Management.* Each of these titles are used by a diversity of approaches toward engaging conflict offered by many consultants, coaches, organization therapists, books, training programs, and other sources. My approach is to suggest that all three of these titles are relevant to engaging conflict, but only at certain intensities.

Conflict Resolution

Conflict Resolution is a process that works best in intensities one and two conflict situations. Resolution, in this context, is all about solutions, probably permanent solutions. It means the specific issues of conflict are resolved and will not have to be engaged again. It is over. In a congregational context the parties have experienced forgiveness and forgetting. Mutual repentance, as appropriate, has occurred, followed by mutual forgiveness. As far as humanly possible, all participants in the conflict are determined to forget about the conflict and move forward.

Genuine resolution happens from the inside out. It cannot be produced by a series of mechanical or organic processes that are carried out in a cultural setting. A person must bring full heart, soul, mind, and strength to resolution for it to be genuine and effective. It is in reality a spiritual process whereby participants are embraced by God's loving presence, and a change of heart occurs. It is an expression of unconditional love, and not love conditioned on the other doing something you want.

Because these are the factors congruent with *Conflict Resolution*, this type of resolution can only happen at intensities one and two. This can occur only when specific issues can be identified. This can occur only when people are willing to own the issues and their parts in the conflict. This can occur only when consensus issue statements can be developed, and working through them becomes the basis for resolution. This can occur only when clear ground rules can quickly be identified and abided by.

Conflict situations of greater intensity cannot be "resolved" at those higher intensities. Only if they can be broken down to their intensity one and two issues can other intensities of conflict be resolved. Once intensity one and two issues are identified, participants may become open to a breakthrough moment from God that will bring forth genuine resolution.

Remember, the theme of intensities one and two is "Getting to *Yes!*" Therefore, the focus should be on getting everyone possible to say "yes" to a positive and productive future for the congregation.

Conflict Mediation

Conflict Mediation is a process that works best at intensities three and four conflict situations. Mediation, in this context, is all about agreements—short-term and long-term agreements that help the congregation move forward. It means the various causes and movements that develop around complex congregational conflict are brought together and agree to a way forward in the midst of the conflict. The agreements are informal and formal, are shared with relevant people and groups, and establish a system for holding one another accountable that is followed.

Mediation does not resolve the specific issues. It provides a plan and a way forward that makes sense for all involved and empowers all parties with new positive energy. It establishes a new temporary foundation for relationship with one another. That foundation can be built upon, or it can remain just a foundation. Additional work must be done to fully resolve the conflict situation.

Following successful mediation, it may be possible to move on to *Conflict Resolution,* through which ultimately true reconciliation might take place. If so, then the processes of resolution can be activated and followed as implied in the paragraphs on *Conflict Resolution.* In other words, it is a two-phase process to engage an intensity three or four conflict situation and end up with resolution.

Conflict Mediation involves tactics such as trust development in personal relationships. Revealing the diverse viewpoints expressed in the bodies of data known as perceived truthful information is a critical part of mediation. In mediation it is difficult to discover truth because both emotions about people and perceptions about facts are highly subjective. A great mediator will be able to bring out the critical emotions and facts that must be revealed for people to acknowledge the beginning point for a way forward.

Remember the theme of intensity three is "Getting to *Yes!*" As with *Conflict Resolution,* the focus should be on getting everyone possible to say "yes" to a positive and productive future for the congregation. However, the theme of intensity four is "Getting Past *No!*" Efforts should be made to prevent participants from carrying the conflict to intensity five because of the highly destructive nature of that intensity.

Conflict Management

Conflict Management is a process that works best at intensities five, six, and seven conflict situations. Management, in this context, is about controlling or directing the situation from the outside because the participants are unable to do so. It means the various individual, groups, and causes in the congregation are compelled or forced to change their behavior or the organization or outside authority will force a change in their behavior.

All processes and agreements are formal. Ground rules and other rules of engagement are partially or wholly required from outside authorities. This is done because intensity five, six, and seven conflict situations are viewed as intractable. They are very difficult to manage. The participants are inflexible, stubborn, volatile, and somewhat unpredictable.

These conflict situations are unhealthy at intensity five, to *severely* unhealthy at intensity seven. At every increasing intensity, the management force must become stronger and able to meet the resistance of the conflict situation participants. Sufficient force at intensity five may prevent the conflict situation from escalating any further. Too often, however, congregations attempt mediation at intensity five, and this proves insufficient to keep the unhealthy conflict intensity from returning with perhaps even greater destructive force.

When an intensity five, six, or seven conflict situation is managed, it is not resolved. If the management is successful and the intensity is de-escalated, the congregation may be ready for some mediation. If that phase is successful, then a resolution process might be engaged and succeed. From management to resolution is a three-phase process. It can also take eighteen to–thirty-six months to fully be realized. It is neither easy nor short.

Remember the theme of intensities five, six, and seven is "Getting to *Neutral!*" which means getting to a place at which a new beginning can occur. Once this new foundation is established, then deeper more meaningful work can occur.

COACHING BREAK

✔ Gaze out the window for a minute. Ponder the situation of your congregation. What images come to mind?

✔ What are examples of the processes for engaging various intensities of conflict that you have used? What was effective about them? What was not effective about them? Do you know what made the difference in some being effective and others not?

✔ How would you explain to someone the differences between *Conflict Resolution, Conflict Mediation,* and *Conflict Management*?

How would you suggest when to use these various processes of engagement? What are the benefits of each?

✔ How would you explain to someone the differences between "Getting to *Yes!*," "Getting Past *No!*," and "Getting to *Neutral!*"? What is the importance of the distinctions between the three? What different types of action do you personally need to be prepared to contribute to each of these themes of intensities of conflict?

Selective Tools for Engaging Conflict

Tools abound for various processes for engaging the intensities of conflict. The goal of this book is not one of repeating or reviewing all the tools available, or of acting as a source book for the tools. The Internet does that so much better and stays more current than this book. However, four tools I have used repeatedly and have molded into my practice of conflict ministry bear some review.

These tools are (1) the congregational life cycle, (2) four pathways to "yes," (3) 100 days of share and prayer triplets, and (4) development of a leadership community to show the way forward.

Implications of the Congregational Life Cycle

For more than thirty years I have been working on a life cycle concept of congregational development. I wrote extensively on it in my book, *Pursuing the Full Kingdom Potential of Your Congregation,* published by Chalice Press of St. Louis in 2006, now part of The Columbia Partnership Leadership Series. You can also find access to my latest thoughts on the congregational life cycle at www. BullardJournal.org. My study has revealed several places in the congregational life cycle at which various kinds of conflict might occur. For reference I have included a copy of this life cycle model at the end of this chapter.

Infancy Stage

The first time conflict becomes a significant issue in a congregation is during the Infancy stage. When a congregation is a couple of years old, they make some adjustments in their identity and practices to conform to the type and style of congregation they are really becoming as compared to the type and style of congregation they thought they were becoming when they launched. This upsets some of the people who were part of the founding. They may determine the congregation is becoming something different than they originally committed to build.

Their reactions are to adjust, leave the congregation, or seek to control the congregation in the direction of the original ministry plan. Their adjustment is the best possible scenario. If they leave well, this is the second best. However, some people may feel they have the right to control the future of the congregation based on the commitment made to them when it was founded. This is usually the worst-case scenario and will require at least some mediation as it may become an intensity three or four conflict.

The hope is the participants in conflict will see this identity and style tension as a typical challenge for congregations in the Infancy stage. Dialogue about this possibility should be part of the founding dialogue concerning the congregation.

Childhood Stage

Too many congregations are not birthed well, with a sufficiently deep sense of spiritual passion about a future toward which God is calling them. Many congregations are franchises of other congregations or their denomination. Others are splits or separation groups from other congregations and are born out of unhealthy conflict. When any of these situations is the case, it is possible for a congregation to experience arrested development during the Childhood stage when they are about six-to-ten years old.

Congregations that experience arrested development and cannot break through this barrier may move across the life cycle to the Retirement stage and not experience the top half of the life cycle. Such a congregation quickly develops institutionalized patterns of existence devoid of vision and assertive disciple-making. In this state they quickly find reasons to be in conflict with one another.

Again, mediation is called for, as the intensity is probably three or four. The focus of the congregation should be on revisioning its spiritual strategic journey as a congregation. Without a clear vision they will be managed by their image of what their former congregation should have been like.

Adolescence Stage

Adolescence is an awkward stage for teenagers. It is also an awkward stage for congregations. Multiple, competing visions tend to be expressed during this stage that confuse the congregation as to the real vision. Business organizations face this same situation. What some of them do is jump what is known as a sigmoid curve to a new life cycle for their organizations. Congregations, however, tend to follow their founding or current vision as much as possible on through to its logical conclusion. While attempting to do that, loud voices in the congregation may be calling for a new movement, a new vision, a new dimension of ministry. This creates in some congregations at least an intensity four conflict situation. In a few it creates an intensity five conflict situation and results in a split in the congregation. Adolescence can be the second-most conflictual stage in the life cycle of a congregation.

Adolescence is a time to formalize the infrastructure that helps the congregation continue moving forward. Congregations are organisms and not organizations. It is typical for them to want to continue a journey in the direction they have already been going for a dozen or more years. Mediation for what probably becomes intensity four conflict is essential.

They can use the conflict as an opportunity to intentionally start one or more new congregations who will ride the crest of the new movements that are emerging in the congregation. They can also begin new worship services, discipleship opportunities, fellowship experiences, and missions and ministry involvements that speak to the new movements and voices.

Empty Nest Stage

The Empty Nest stage is the most conflictual stage in the life of the congregation. It is the stage that begins with nostalgia about the past, and regrets that the congregation is not what it once was. This then moves to a disappointment that it is failing in comparison to the past. The response to the disappointment is for a core group of people to push the concept of commitment and suggest that everyone simply needs to work harder and be more committed.

The third phase of Empty Nest is the anger phase, in which leaders and followers both look for something or someone to blame for why they are not what they used to be. Often this blaming ultimately turns in the direction of the current pastor. When this happens, the intensity of conflict often moves to at least four, if not five. A conflict management consultant must be brought in to deal with the conflict situation. When it gets to this stage, more times than not the pastor is terminated formally or through pressure on denominational officials who have authority in this area.

Such congregations could bypass the anger phase if they were able to realize the nostalgia phase and start working to redevelop forward to a new partial life cycle at this juncture. Congregations in the Empty Nest stage are no longer being driven by God's vision for their future. Rather than being led into the future, they are seeking to manage into the future.

Retirement Stage

Some congregations panic during the Retirement stage. They realize they are not what they once were and are not fulfilling their dreams as a congregation. Yet they do not know what to do. They have no vision and feel they are lacking energy they once had. Many of their leaders are older. What they hope is that they can secure through a call or appointment system—according to the polity of their denomination—a pastor who will come to the congregation with a clear sense of vision for the future and work hard to live into that future.

Because this is their stance, they place a lot of responsibility and accountability on the new pastor. Too often these congregations get into a pattern of short pastorates of no more than four years. A new pastor comes and tries new things. They either do not work or do not work in the manner the lay leaders would like to see. Then the pastor is pressured to leave or is terminated outright, and they call a new pastor.

Obviously, these congregations can fall into an unhealthy pattern of intensity five conflicts. They become repeat offenders. As such, they need an outside conflict management consultant or arbitrator to help them break their unhealthy pattern. They are unlikely to call on such a person until they are feeling a strong sense of desperation, or some incident triggers their need for such intervention.

In general, both Empty Nest and Retirement congregations are susceptible to unhealthy conflict. The key missing ingredient in these congregations is a strong, positive sense of God's spiritual strategic direction. In a word, it is the lack of vision that haunts them. For these congregations, and all the others in the life cycle stages mentioned here, proactive assessment of congregations according to the life cycle stages will prepare congregations to deal with what can be close to inevitable crises in their lives as Christ-centered, faith-based communities.

Four Pathways to **Yes!**

"Four Pathways to *Yes!*" is superior to a problem-solving approach that focuses on where participants disagree rather than where they agree. Seeking pathways to *Yes!* is a collaborative model that can build a leadership community with the capacity to handle many opportunities and challenges. It can be effective up through intensity four conflict situations.

Here are the "Four Pathways to *Yes!*" The goal is to increasingly find ways to say "yes" rather than "no" to the opportunities and challenges a congregation faces. Problem-solving approaches fix what is negative. This collaborative model seeks to discover perhaps already existing affirmation for the next steps of a congregation's ministry.

Pathway One: I can say Yes! to some or all of the proposal or ideas right now.

Often you can reach immediate agreement on many aspects of a proposal or idea. These early wins should be affirmed from the beginning and throughout the dialogue.

Each round of dialogue should assume the depth of consensus already achieved. Participants should be held accountable for the decisions in those areas where they have affirmed the proposal or idea.

Pathway Two: I can say Yes! to the proposal or idea if I have more information.

Frequently the presenters of a new proposal or idea do not provide enough background information or do not know the information most desired by participants in the decision-making process. Or, participants want to ask questions to assure themselves that various perspectives or interests have been included in the development of the proposal or idea.

Also, if a new proposal or idea develops in the midst of dialogue, it usually will require more information to discover any systemic impact it may have on the individual or organization.

Pathway Three: I can say Yes! to the proposal or idea if I have more time for dialogue.

Persons presented with a new proposal or idea often have a *process deficit*. They have not had the same time or opportunity to process the proposal or idea as have the presenters.

By providing time and good facilitation to those receiving a proposal, it is possible that saying *Yes!* to the proposal or idea will be possible within a reasonable amount of time. Also, if a new proposal or idea develops in the midst of dialogue, it may require significant dialogue and facilitation to build a consensus.

Pathway Four: I cannot say *Yes!* to the proposal or idea in its current form, but I would be open to future dialogue.
Some people have legitimate problems with a given proposal or idea. They need to be able to express that they are not prepared to say *Yes!* without being the focus of disapproval from the remainder of the group.

Often their inability to say *Yes!* is because they need additional information or dialogue. At times it is because the proposal appears to violate their core values. When core values are violated, saying *Yes!* can be tough and involve *soul-searching* efforts to reevaluate previously nonnegotiable perspectives.

100 Days of Share and Prayer Triplets

For fifteen years I have been working with a concept known as *100 Days of Share and Prayer Triplets.* As with the congregational life cycle section above, I have written about this in my book, *Pursuing the Full Kingdom Potential of Your Congregation,* and have up-to-date materials on it available through www.BullardJournal.org. Rather than go into the details of the *100 Days of Share and Prayer Triplets,* I would refer you to chapter 7 of my earlier book and to this Web address. A few essential elements of the application of these triplets in conflict ministry would be appropriate.

I typically seek to form share and prayer triplets in congregations in which I am serving as a conflict management consultant. They are experiencing at least an intensity four conflict situation. There may be signs they are preparing for an intensity five conflict event, or they may have recently experienced such an event.

Once I have made an assessment of their situation and offered strong recommendations to them, I typically lead them in a period of healing and reconciliation along with other activities. During this time I propose they form share and prayer triplets. Each triplet (group of three people) would be composed of people who have mild to radically different viewpoints from one another on the conflict situation of the congregation.

During 100 days they are asked to meet ten times for up to 100 minutes each time for fellowship, dialogue, and prayer concerning their congregational situation. Typically they have misconceptions about one another, and differing perspectives on the opportunities and challenges facing the congregation. Following these 100 days, people often discover they share more common ground than had been predicted. This can often set the stage to move from conflict management to conflict mediation, and the de-escalation of the conflict by one intensity.

By the way, each triplet is brought together by a member of the leadership community whose formation is described in the next section.

Developing a Leadership Community

Part of my philosophy of helping congregations with their conflict and challenges is to suggest people of key influence in their congregation need to be brought together and challenged to lead the way forward. These would include people from various perspectives on the conflict. This is a strategy for intensity four and five conflict situations. The initial key step is identifying these people. Here is how I do it.

First, I ask every person I talk to in a congregation to list for me on a survey form their personal top ten people in the life of the congregation who have the greatest amount of influence on the direction and culture of the congregation. Upfront I tell them they must sign their list and own their affirmation of these people as key influencers. I also indicate that I am the only one who is going to see these lists, and that when I am finished with them I will destroy the lists.

Second, I ask them to look back over their list and rate the manner in which each of these ten people expresses their influence by three categories—easygoing, strong, and overbearing. People who express their influence in an easygoing way *may* cause people to be aware of their influence. They are pleasant, calm, helpful, insightful, positive, and their influence enhances relationships.

Everyone is aware of the influence of people whose influence is strong. They are powerful, persuasive, outspoken, highly competent, still generally positive, but do not necessarily enhance relationships.

People who express their influence in an overbearing manner are known by everyone, highly respected, followed by some, and barely tolerated by others. They are controlling, dominating, blunt, less competent than they think, negative, and angry. Many times it would be better if they remained quiet because when they speak up people are naturally put off by them.

Third, I ask them once again to review their list and choose three of the ten people who they feel are most trustworthy to be part of a leadership community who will seek to find a way forward for the congregation. Trust is the key concept and the highest valued currency of conflict ministry.

After gathering these surveys, I compile them. My compilation reveals several things. First, it reveals the people who are perceived to have the greatest amount of influence in the life and ministry of the congregation. The compilation makes this obvious as I list people from the most frequently mentioned to the least frequently mentioned. Second, it culls from the list the influential people who are perceived as overbearing. Usually there is about one per hundred in average attendance of adults in a congregation. Third, it reveals the people among the most influential people who are not perceived as being overbearing but are seen as the most trustworthy.

These are the people among whom I form a leadership community to work with me as the conflict management consultant in the congregation. In my covenant with the congregation I have stated that I get to choose the people who work with me to manage the conflict situation. These are the ones.

For clarity and review, they are the people who are perceived to have the greatest amount of influence in the life and ministry of the congregation, whose manner of influence is not perceived to be overbearing, and who are perceived as highly trustworthy to be part of a leadership community to find a way forward.

From this compiled list, I choose the people with the following criteria. First, I choose a minimum twelve people, and a maximum of thirty-five people, depending on the attendance size of the congregation. If for any reason the pastor and key staff minister or staff program leaders are not ranked high on the list, I automatically include them. If both a husband and wife are highly ranked on the list, I only choose one, and often choose the wife to provide some sense of gender equity.

One more time let me be sure you notice that highly influential people who are overbearing and not trustworthy are excluded from the process. For many of them this is a humbling experience, and because the congregation chose the people by means of my survey, something they are unable to oppose.

If these people chosen for the leadership community can get their act together about a positive way forward for the congregation, the congregation will generally follow, and, if they follow, will seldom return to an unhealthy intensity of conflict for many years to come.

COACHING INSIGHTS

■ Before reading this chapter, how did you view processes for engaging the intensities of conflict? How do you view them now? What had been your experience in working with various processes for engaging conflict?

■ In what stage of the congregational life cycle is your congregation today? What types of conflict situations can you anticipate or even prevent because you know where you are in the life cycle? What steps do you need to take very soon to address potential or existing conflict?

■ How do you visualize conflict? Is it a problem to solve or an opportunity to address? Do you focus on what divides or on what unites? How can the "Four Pathways to *Yes!*" help you address conflict situations differently and more positively?

■ What potential do you see in your congregation for the empowerment toward solutions that is represented in the share and prayer triplet process? When and how will you use this tool in your congregation?

■ Do you know who forms the leadership community of key influencers in your congregation according to the criteria shared in this chapter? Is this a group you could survey the congregation to discover and bring together, or do you need an outside third party to facilitate that process for you?

PERSONAL REFLECTIONS

Your Reflections: What are your reflections on the material presented in this chapter?

_____

_____

_____

_____

Your Actions: What actions do you need to take about your life, ministry, and/or congregation based on the material presented in this chapter?

_____

_____

_____

_____

Your Accountability: How and by whom do you want to be held accountable for taking these actions?

_____

_____

_____

_____

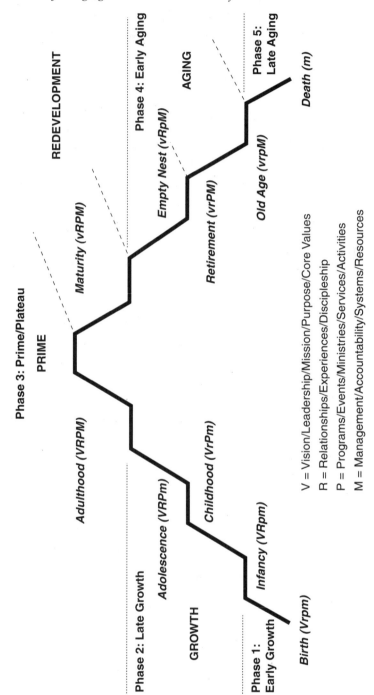

Phase 3: Prime/Plateau

PRIME

REDEVELOPMENT

Phase 4: Early Aging

AGING

Phase 5: Late Aging

Maturity (vRPM)

Empty Nest (vRpM)

Retirement (vrPM)

Old Age (vrpM)

Death (m)

Adulthood (VRPM)

Phase 2: Late Growth

Adolescence (VRPm)

Childhood (VrPm)

GROWTH

Infancy (VRpm)

Phase 1: Early Growth

Birth (Vrpm)

V = Vision/Leadership/Mission/Purpose/Core Values
R = Relationships/Experiences/Discipleship
P = Programs/Events/Ministries/Services/Activities
M = Management/Accountability/Systems/Resources

11

How to Never Experience Unhealthy Conflict in Your Congregation Again

EXECUTIVE SUMMARY

The purpose of this chapter is to dialogue about how to proactively work to avoid unhealthy conflict in your congregation because you are embraced by a vision and spiritual strategic journey that is greater than many issues of conflict. The focus is on hardwiring into your congregational culture the processes necessary to insulate your congregation from the destructive force present in the midst of unhealthy conflict.

Let's be honest. I have no way to guarantee you will never experience unhealthy conflict in your congregation again. Ways do exist for you to inoculate yourself against it. But no way carries a 100 percent guarantee. Things happen that cause unhealthy conflict. At times these occur without warning. Other times things do not happen that should have happened, things that, if they had, would have—could have—kept you from experiencing unhealthy conflict situations. What follows is a list of twenty things you can intentionally do in your congregation that may inoculate you from experiencing unhealthy conflict.

Twenty Things to Do to Never Experience Unhealthy Conflict in Your Congregation

1. Develop a clear core ideology involving mission, purpose, and theological and cultural values, a magnetic God-given vision, and an appealing future story for the life and ministry of your congregation into which you are seeking to live. Doing these things will leave little room for unhealthy conflict situations and will empower the congregation forward into an exciting future.

2. Every eight to ten years renew your core ideology and revision your compelling vision. Plan major new strategies every three to five years. Renew the operational plan continually, but always looking eighteen to thirty-six months into the future. Every 120 days update your future story to keep it relevant and congruent to what God is actually doing in and through your congregation.

3. Create a conflict-literate culture in your congregation by engaging in conflict ministry education within the congregation involving the pastoral and staff leadership and people of passion and people of position, which is known as your enduring visionary leadership community. (See chapter 3 of my book, Pursuing the Full Kingdom Potential of Your Congregation.)

4. Create a "FaithSoaring" culture in your congregation that believes congregations must walk by faith rather than by sight, in the spirit of 2 Corinthians 5:7. Believe that in such a culture it is a positive thing to work through healthy conflicts as a means to be prepared to handle potentially unhealthy conflict situations. All the time, focus on what is good, loving, and right about the congregation rather than what is bad, hateful, and wrong.

5. Hardwire into your congregational culture that you always seek outside third-party assistance when conflict in your congregation reaches intensity four. For crucial staff-related issues, bring in an outside third-party by intensity three. The reason is that senior pastors and staff ministers have a tendency to escalate conflict too quickly, and so they often need assistance sooner than laypersons do.

6. Develop and implement open, healthy decision-making processes in your congregation that involve a lot of people in owning decisions and being committed to necessary actions. Always keep your decision-making processes open to new ideas, movements, and spiritual opportunities. Always renew your governing documents and policies at least every five years. Even develop a sunset clause in your policies that they expire unless renewed every five years.

7. Develop and implement open, healthy communication processes in your congregation that have redundancy of communication, feedback loops, and use a variety of communication vehicles. In this way you can be sure people are not left out because they do not read the newsletter, do not listen to the announcements in worship, or do not have or will not read their e-mail. It is often an illusion that full communication has occurred. Or, the belief that full communication has occurred is often an illusion. Get it?

8. Deal with all conflict situations based on principles consistent with the core ideology of the congregation, and not based on partisan positions or personalities. Principles will affirm the core ideology of your congregation and keep you centered on the things that are most important. Conflict finds many open doors when principles are discarded for political expediency or to yield to the strength and controlling tactics of a personality.

9. Realize processes that are open, healthy, and respected are as important as the principles being upheld. Therefore, people who approach conflict by position, and shut out good process, are the enemies of healthy congregations. Often moral or theological issues become emotional issues in which people tend to throw out what would otherwise be wise counsel concerning process.

10. Senior pastors and staff ministers need coaching by an outside third-party by the time conflict reaches intensity three. The same may be true for key laypersons who get drawn into conflict situations, or are the antagonists in these situations. It is not a bad idea—in fact, it is a great idea—for the pastor and staff ministers to have a personal ministry coach all the time. It is also a great idea for these staff persons to be trained as coaches and use their experience and skills as a leadership tactic in the congregation.

11. Senior pastors and staff ministers need a BAMP. This stands for a Best Alternative Ministry Placement. It means if the current conflict situation does not work out, what is the best alternative ministry placement for each minister to continue in Christian ministry service? If pastors and staff ministers have this thought through and worked out, they can remain engaged in conflict situations longer and with a healthier sense of accomplishment. They can remain healthier spiritually, emotionally, and physically. (This idea is based on the concept of BATNA—Best Alternative to a Negotiated Agreement—which I first encountered in a book by Roger Fisher and William Ury, entitled *Getting to Yes: Negotiating Agreement Without Giving In* [New York: Penguin Press, 1981], pp. 101–111.)

12. Senior pastors and staff ministers need to have a personal mission statement and future story of their ministry that projects beyond their current place of service, is not dependent on it, and definitely sees beyond any current conflict situation. It is difficult for senior pastors and staff ministers to lead congregations to have a core ideology, vision, and future story if they have not worked through a similar process for their own ministry.

13. Congregations should have well-written governing documents and policies that activate to deal with any approaching unhealthy conflict situations. Sections of the documents should suggest what should happen if conflict arises in the life and ministry of the congregation. It is hoped these policies and procedures will be based on healthy models of governance and not simply a reaction to how such a situation was handled badly in the past.

14. All congregational leaders need to learn how not to fall into the trap of escalating conflict unnecessarily. Pastors and staff ministers in particular can be guilty of such unnecessary escalation. Overreaction is the enemy of congregations. Taking a single issue and expanding it to cover a multitude of issues says a lot more about the person who escalates the conflict than it does about the people being accused.

15. Congregations should learn how to embrace diversity of viewpoints, theology, culture, socioeconomics, birth generations, and tenure in the congregation consistent with its core ideology. Congregations that require harmony in these areas will be disrupted by diversity and experience unhealthy

conflict. To handle diversity, congregations need to learn the art of dialogue rather than the science of discussion and debate.

16. Develop and implement an ongoing prayer culture in the life and ministry of the congregation in which members pray for one another, pray for the life and ministry of the congregation, pray for the clergy and lay leaders, and pray that the Evil One will find no place of comfort in this congregation. Congregations who earnestly pray for one another find they have less they dislike about one another.

17. Congregations who focus on adult discipleship development that includes discovery of the spiritual gifts, life skills, and personality preferences of its congregational participants and mobilizes them in mission and ministry based on this will be too much on mission to be disrupted by unhealthy conflict. Mobilization is the new assimilation. When new people genuinely are made to feel a part of the congregation, then long-tenured people will not be threatened by them and ignite unnecessary conflict.

18. Congregations who regularly have fun with one another are healthier congregations emotionally. Regularly means having some type of significant community building experiences at least ten times per year that can involve the whole congregation. Interaction, fellowship, and koinonia are critical characteristics of healthy congregations. This can also contribute to spiritual health. It provides a great defense against unhealthy conflict.

19. Just as in marriages, one of the top three sources of conflict is money; so, if a congregation is struggling financially, this provides an open door for unhealthy conflict. To avoid unhealthy conflict, include a regular proactive emphasis on financial stewardship in the perennial programs of your congregation. Have financial procedures and practices that are beyond reproach. Report regularly to the congregation the state of the finances.

20. Take intentional actions to insulate the congregation, but especially its clergy leaders, against legal, moral, and ethical failures. Numerous issues within this trilogy of issues can explode onto the scene of a congregation and create unhealthy conflict before anyone has an opportunity to take preventative actions. At times this explosion can occur because of an accusation that may later prove to be untrue. It does not matter. The damage is done.

COACHING BREAK

✔ Gaze out the window for a minute. Ponder the situation of your congregation. What images come to mind?

✔ Do you believe it is possible to inoculate your congregation against unhealthy conflict? What would be the barriers to this inoculation? Have you ever experienced such a congregation? If so, do you see this as unique, or could you see it happening again?

✔ Of the twenty things listed, which ones make the most sense to you? Where is your congregation as far as this list of twenty? How many are fully true of your congregation? How many are partially true? How many are not true at all?

✔ Do you disagree with any of these? Which ones? Why? Do you have other ones with which to replace them?

What Is the Value of a Vision and a Spiritual Strategic Journey?

From my viewpoint, three of the twenty items listed in the first part of this chapter that help in the inoculation process against unhealthy conflict are key, nonnegotiable items. They are numbers one, three, and twenty. Many of the others are extremely important. Some of them are likely to take place anyway if you focus on these three.

Number twenty is important because these issues represent an explosion of conflict when they occur. When any change factor in a congregation happens so fast that you have no reaction time, then it is less likely you will be able to adjust to it. In addition, legal, moral, or ethical failure pushes our emotional hot buttons so easily. We often do not use good, loving process to respond in these situations.

Number three is important because too many congregations and their leaders are illiterate when it comes to conflict ministry. Effective conflict ministry education alone would keep many congregational leaders and clergy from escalating unnecessarily the inevitable conflicts that occur.

Of all the possible actions that could be taken, however, number one is the most effective. I have been teaching conflict ministry for twenty-five years now. I have been consulting off and on for almost twenty years with congregations who would acknowledge from the beginning that their primary issue was one of conflict. Congregations with whom I have worked during that time who have fully embraced number one have not experienced unhealthy conflict since.

Congregations who stopped short of developing a clear core ideology, vision, and future story have experienced unhealthy conflict again. In fact, some never stopped experiencing it after I completed my work with them.

Therefore, the value of a vision and spiritual strategic journey is priceless. The cost in time, effort, and money of doing it is nominal in comparison with the benefits of living into a spiritual strategic journey. (The spiritual strategic journey process is fully described in my book *Pursuing the Full Kingdom Potential of Your Congregation*, and updates can be found at www.BullardJournal.org.)

The spiritual strategic journey process takes approximately one year to become hardwired into the life and ministry of a congregation. It is a relational approach to planning that is strategic in nature. It seeks to empower a large number of people in the congregation to own the future story of the congregation.

Why does this work as a preventative to unhealthy conflict?

I have often said that I have never had the opportunity to work in conflict management with a congregation that has a clear core ideology, vision, and future story. The reason is that conflict is incompatible with this situation. Congregations who know who they are, where they are headed, and how they are getting there have no room for unhealthy conflict.

The opposite is also true. Of the congregations I have worked with in conflict management, none of them knew who they were, where they were headed, or how they were going to get there. If they had known, they probably would have handled their conflict situation effectively themselves and not needed to call me for assistance.

To answer the question I posed, this works because vision and a spiritual strategic journey provide focus, motivation, and empowerment for congregations. Further, they are collectively walking with God. Thus they have great room for empowerment, but no room for control, great opportunities to add value to the congregation, but no room to steal value away from the congregation.

COACHING INSIGHTS

■ Before reading this chapter, did you think it was possible to never experience unhealthy conflict in your congregation again? What do you think now? If you still believe this is impossible, what is the evidence you would share? If you believe this is possible, what is the evidence?

■ Do you believe that a core ideology, vision, and future story that is deeply owned and lived out in a congregation is the key factor to never experiencing unhealthy conflict again? If yes, why? If no, why?

■ What steps would you need to take to develop or reveal the core ideology, vision, and future story of your congregation? What should be your next steps over the next thirty, sixty, and ninety days to do this? Who is ready to help you? Who else will you need to recruit?

■ Does your congregation have a disaster communication plan to handle surprise announcements about legal, moral, or ethical failures of key clergy and laity in your congregation? If not, what do you need to do to develop one? It does not have to be formal. It simply needs to be effective for your situation.

■ What have you done, or what plans could you make, to engage in conflict ministry education of the leadership of your congregation? When will you plan to do this? Who will you ask to help you with the training?

PERSONAL REFLECTIONS

Your Reflections: What are your reflections on the material presented in this chapter?

Your Actions: What actions do you need to take about your life, ministry, and/or congregation based on the material presented in this chapter?

_____

_____

_____

_____

Your Accountability: How and by whom do you want to be held accountable for taking these actions?

_____

_____

_____

_____

12

Implications for Denominational Service alongside Congregations

EXECUTIVE SUMMARY

The purpose of this chapter is to dialogue about the role of denominational organizations and denominational staff in coming alongside congregations throughout the intensities of conflict. It will provide a process for coming alongside congregations during times of healthy and unhealthy conflict.

Every denominational organization finds itself spending a lot of time dealing with its own conflicts and the conflicts present within its congregations. It is inevitable because as indicated in the introduction to this book, conflict is the number one growth industry for Christian congregations. Denominations who seek to avoid conflict do so at great peril.

Too many denominational organizations have an inadequate approach to conflict in their affiliated congregations. They respond only when they see no other choice. Or, they offer conflict resolution and mediation approaches that are ineffective beyond intensity three to four conflict situations.

Or, they take what they think is a proactive approach of equipping their staff to handle conflict situations, and the result is that hard-working staff persons develop the skill of seeing dysfunction or conflict in every congregational situation, so the incidents of conflict increase and overload the staff. Or, they involve themselves too soon or too frequently in congregation conflict, and they actually escalate conflict and create perpetually unhealthy and dysfunctional congregational systems.

What Denominations Need to Do

Denominations need to do the following fifteen things concerning the existence of conflict in the congregations in their area, district, middle judicatory, region, or national organization.

1. *Admit denominations* probably cannot significantly help very many congregations. You cannot let yourself get messianic about helping congregations with their conflicts. You cannot become blinded by a rescuer mentality that seeks to help the un-help-able. Unhealthy conflict is hardwired into the culture of too many congregations.

2. *Model healthy conflict* ministry in the denominational ministry and operations. This would be a great accomplishment for denominations. It would also be one that has eluded denominations throughout their history. A national, regional, or local denominational body who is a model of healthy conflict ministry is difficult to find, and, if found, difficult to sustain. It seems odd that some denominational structures and staff place expectations on congregations and on their leaders that the denomination finds difficult to model itself.

3. *Work with receptive congregations* on developing within their fellowship a clear ideology involving mission and purpose, a captivating vision, and an appealing future story of ministry around which they are seeking to live. When congregations have this, they are less likely to allow room for unhealthy conflict. They find ways to work through many conflict situations.

4. *Create a conflict-literate culture* in your denominational organization by engaging in conflict ministry education. Involve your key employed, elected, and appointed leadership. Hardwire healthy conflict ministry processes into your culture and into the culture of your congregations.

5. *Create a positive culture* in your denomination that believes it is a good thing to work through healthy conflicts. Do this as

a preparation for handling the inevitable unhealthy conflict situations. This can significantly increase the capacity of denominations and their congregations to handle complex conflict situations.

6. *Hardwire into your denominational culture that outside assistance is always sought when conflict reaches intensity four.* Seeking outside assistance is seen as an admission of failure in some organizational systems. Do not buy into this concept. Rather, model for congregations the advantages of asking for help when needed.

7. *Develop and implement open, healthy decision-making processes within the denominational organization.* A great way to inoculate an organizational system against unhealthy conflict is education and practice at handling healthy decision-making, thus developing the capacity in leadership to handle potential unhealthy conflict situations.

8. *Offer to help develop and implement open, healthy communication systems within congregations.* In many congregations, internal communication patterns are inadequate. When communication systems are inadequate, congregational participants develop their own story as to what is going on, because they feel left out and unappreciated. This ultimately creates suspicion of leaders.

9. *Deal with conflict situations based on principles rather than positions.* Model for congregations how conflict is handled based on principles, core values, and healthy processes. Too many conflict situations are handled based on personality, position, and power—laying the groundwork for unhealthy conflict.

10. *Realize process that is open, healthy, and respected is as important as the principles of conflict.* Therefore, people who approach conflict by position also tend not to follow good process. Great principles and core values can be undermined by poor process. Great process treats all as persons of worth created in the image of God to live and to love. Poor process treats people as opponents who need to lose.

11. *Develop relationships with clergy and key lay leadership that allow you to speak into their conflict situations as they arise.* It is difficult to assist congregations with their conflict situations if the denominational staff does not know the clergy and key lay leadership as fellow Christians, ministry colleagues, and friends. Speaking out of a depth of relationships will empower

Persuade, Collaborate, and *Negotiate* as conflict leadership styles available for use by denominational staff.

12. *Pastors and staff ministers need to be coached by an outside third party by the time conflict reaches intensity three.* Because of the tendency of pastors and staff ministers to escalate conflict once it reaches intensity three, the denomination should make available to them coaching by an outside third party to assist them in maintaining good process at a time of personal threat. Denominational staff may serve as these coaches in some situations.

13. *Pastors and staff ministers need to have a clear alternative future.* Pastors and staff ministers must discern, discover, develop, and maintain a clear alternative future for their ministry. Such a clear alternative future revolves around the question, "If ministry in this setting does not work out or comes to an abrupt end, what would I do?" Having a clear alternative future allows pastors and staff ministers to remain engaged longer with lower stress in many situations of conflict in their ministry setting. Denominations should assist clergy in developing a clear alternative future.

14. *Pastors and staff ministers need to have a future story that goes beyond their current place of service and sees way beyond current circumstances.* Even stronger than a clear alternative future, which focuses on what a person would do next, is a long-term future story of ministry. What does a pastor or staff minister see as his or her long-term ministry goals and legacy? Denominations can help clergy craft such stories.

15. *Learn how not to fall into the trap of escalating conflict unnecessarily.* The intervention of denominations into congregational conflict can easily escalate the intensity of conflict, if the intervention is too strong or too direct for the intensity of conflict. Therefore, denominational staff need to understand the intensities of conflict and the processes of conflict to know how to intervene in a helpful rather than hurtful manner.

COACHING BREAK

✔ Gaze out the window for a minute. Ponder the situation of your denomination. What images come to mind?

✔ How does your denomination handle various intensities of conflict in its own organizational life? Does it follow a healthy process? Is it principle-based or positional? Is it based on controlling the denomination and its affiliated congregations, or empowering them?

✔ What is your track record in working with your affiliated congregations as they experience various intensities of conflict? Have you had a proactive strategy or a reactive strategy?

A Denominational Conflict Ministry Strategy Proposal

The following is a proposed conflict ministry strategy for a newly emerging denomination that has been in existence for around a decade. As this denomination is developing its various systems, it has gotten to the point that it needs a process of conflict ministry. Existing denominations would do well to image themselves as a newly emerging denomination without a formal approach to conflict ministry, and then to discern, discover, and develop the system that will work within their denominational ethos.

I call the denomination in this proposal the Missional Denomination. It is a denomination with polity in which clergy are accountable to denominational hierarchy in addition to being accountable to their local congregations.

The Missional Denomination is an emerging denomination seeking to develop various patterns of service and management for its affiliated congregations. One of these is in the area of conflict ministry. It is hoped and desired that such matters can be resolved within the fellowship of a local congregation following biblical principles, including those prescribed in Matthew 18.

Currently the informal system involves a denominational staff person in every conflict situation in which knowledge of a conflict expands beyond the local congregation. Each situation may also involve numerous networks within the Missional Denomination in dialogue, and emotional involvement in each situation. The network ministers, the name given to the regional staff persons, are particularly at a disadvantage when they must involve themselves in internal congregational conflict rather than providing spiritual and strategic leadership for their assigned congregations.

Congregations need help developing the capacity to deal with many of their low intensity, healthy conflict situations. Networks of congregations need help developing mediation processes that will assist in mid-intensity, healthy to transitional conflict situations.

The overarching challenge is to engage appropriate conflict situations in congregations through an overall conflict ministry approach that addresses necessary issues. It may also focus on helping congregations and the Missional Denomination move in the direction of their full Kingdom potential. Unhealthy conflict is a hindrance to response to the Great Commission in the spirit of the Great Commandment, so there is an urgency to address a comprehensive approach to conflict ministry.

One possible solution to this challenge is for the Missional Denomination to develop a system to provide comprehensive *Conflict Ministry*. Such services would allow the denomination to stay focused on its core spiritual strategic journey, use respected leaders within the denomination to work with congregations, and use a third party for coaching the process and addressing intensity four and higher conflict ministry situations.

This would be an overall *Conflict Ministry* approach rather than just a *Conflict Resolution* approach. The difference is that a *Conflict Resolution* approach has the tendency to focus on obtaining a fix for a given conflict situation so it will no longer exist. True resolution happens very infrequently. *Conflict Ministry* recognizes that conflict is a typical part of everyday life in a congregation. We must learn how to accept and even be empowered by healthy conflict. We must learn how to mediate mid-intensity conflict, and how to manage unhealthy conflict.

Conflict Ministry Architecture

The *Conflict Ministry* architecture could include the following elements: oversight, education, assessment, mediation, and management. While this represents an initial proposed plan, as the Missional Denomination grows and matures, this architecture will need to be continually modified.

Oversight

An overall *Conflict Ministry* architecture should be developed in cooperation with the leadership of the Missional Denomination. An assigned staff person, perhaps called a conflict ministry coordinator, should provide oversight to this ministry.

The goal of the oversight aspect of this architecture is to provide overall guidance for a proactive and healthy *Conflict Ministry* approach for the Missional Denomination that honors the supervision and accountability inherent in a system in which all clergy come under authority.

Education

The Missional Denomination should engage in a proactive *Conflict Ministry* education process focused on helping clergy and laity become aware of various aspects and approaches to conflict ministry and develop tools for engaging in *Conflict Ministry*. The ideal would be for this to be done within the various networks throughout the denomination.

This education would involve the development of education events or learning experiences for congregational and denominational leaders on *Conflict Readiness*. These events would focus on an overall understanding of conflict, a general understanding as to what to expect at various intensities of conflict, and a specific understanding of getting congregations and networks ready to deal with conflict, with a special emphasis on what can be done in congregations to deal with intensity one and two conflict situations in which *Conflict Resolution* is a real possibility.

Levels of Education

Three levels of education would form this aspect (with a fourth that could be added later). These levels are *Conflict Ministry Awareness* education, *Conflict Resolution* education, and *Conflict Mediation* education.

Conflict Ministry Awareness Education

Conflict Ministry Awareness education would seek to acquaint any and all congregational and denominational leaders concerning *Conflict Ministry*. It would seek to suggest some common language and processes that could be used in any congregation or other situation.

Conflict Ministry Awareness education would take six classroom hours.

Conflict Resolution Education

Conflict Resolution education would be available for congregational and denominational leaders who are likely to be directly involved in *Conflict Ministry* and need a deeper understanding of the dynamics necessary to lead in the midst of intensities one, two, three, and four conflict. The focus would be on proactively dealing with intensities one and two conflict with the goal of *Conflict Resolution*.

Ideally every pastor, clergy staff, and board officer should have this training available to them. *Conflict Resolution* education would take twelve classroom hours, and would have *Conflict Ministry Awareness* education as a prerequisite. In addition, three months should have passed since participants attended *Conflict Ministry Awareness* education.

Conflict Mediation Education

Conflict Mediation education would be available for network, area, or district leaders, any persons on *Conflict Ministry* teams, and denominational leaders. The content would deal with intensities three, four, and five conflict. The focus would be on proactively dealing with intensities three and four conflicts when *Conflict Mediation* may effectively handle conflict situations while they are still healthy or transitional.

Conflict Mediation education would take twelve classroom hours and would have *Conflict Ministry Awareness* and *Conflict Resolution* education as prerequisites. In addition, three months should have passed since participants attended *Conflict Resolution* education.

The goal of the education aspect of this architecture is to equip the Missional Denomination congregational and denominational leaders to be ready to deal with the various inevitable conflict situations that are part of congregational and denominational life.

Conflict Management Education

A fourth level of education can be offered at a later date. This would be *Conflict Management* education. This would be education available by invitation only by the Missional Denomination conflict ministry coordinator. It is intended to develop the denominational leaders who can ultimately handle 90 percent of the *Conflict Ministry* processes, with a minimal involvement of outside assistance.

This education would be for a minimum of three people and a maximum of seven people at a time. The education process would take one year. It would involve beginning with sixteen classroom hours, a practicum in *Conflict Ministry*, six months of coaching, and then a follow-up learning experience of sixteen classroom hours. Those who complete this process could be certified by The Columbia Partnership at www.TheColumbiaPartnership.org as *Conflict Ministry Coaches*.

Conflict Ministry Awareness, Conflict Resolution, and *Conflict Mediation* education are prerequisites. In addition, three months should have passed since participants attended *Conflict Mediation* education.

Assessment

The Missional Denomination should provide *Conflict Ministry Assessment* services to its congregations when they have a conflict situation that is at intensity three or higher and feel they do not have sufficient capacity to handle their conflict situation without it escalating and harming mission. These assessment or triage services should be provided by respected and trustworthy clergy and lay leaders appointed by the conflict ministry coordinator, and accountable only to this person.

Congregations can request this *Conflict Ministry Assessment* service. A network can request the *Conflict Ministry Assessment* service on behalf of and with the concurrence of both the pastor and the board chairperson. Network, area, or district leaders can request the *Conflict Ministry Assessment* service with the knowledge of the pastor and board chairperson that they are requesting this service.

The aim of *Conflict Ministry Assessment* is to determine what, if any, intervention is needed into a congregation to effectively deal with the issues of conflict that confront it in such a way as to empower mission and diffuse, mediate, and perhaps resolve issues of conflict that are hindering mission fulfillment. Recommendations are made as to what actions need to be taken to address the conflict situation, and to determine whether these actions can be handled within the congregation, within the network, in partnership with another network, or if they require third-party *Conflict Management* intervention.

The goal of the assessment aspect of this architecture is to develop a resource within the Missional Denomination for quickly assessing conflict situations within congregations so that these situations may be addressed, and mission may be fulfilled rather than derailed.

Mediation

The Missional Denomination should provide *Conflict Mediation* services to its congregations when they have a conflict situation that is at intensity three or greater and feel they do not have sufficient capacity to handle their conflict situation without it escalating and harming mission. Such services should be preceded by a *Conflict Ministry Assessment* that engages in triage activities to determine the service that would fit the need of the congregation.

Conflict Mediation services can be provided by various persons or entities. First would be by the people available to engage in

Conflict Ministry Assessment services who may also have been trained in *Conflict Mediation*. A small risk exists that those who do the assessment may already have formed opinions that would make it difficult—but not impossible—to be neutral process mediators.

Second could be one or more persons within the network, area, or district who have been trained in *Conflict Mediation*. A medium risk exists that those who are within the same judicatory may have difficulty remaining neutral, may be barraged with information about the conflict that interferes with the mediation, and may compromise their long-term relationship with other denominational leaders and congregational members within the particular network if the mediation does not go extremely well.

Third could be one or more persons from another judicatory who have been trained in *Conflict Mediation*. While some small risks still exist, this is probably the best of the three alternatives mentioned here. There is enough distance to substantially maintain neutrality. There is enough familiarity with the ideology and dynamics of a congregation that they do not have to learn the Missional Denomination culture. It also can be a tremendous learning experience as they consider conflict situations in their own judicatory and how they can develop healthy patterns of dealing with them.

The goal of the mediation aspect of this architecture is to help congregations with mid-intensity conflict situations effectively deal with these situations before they become unhealthy, dysfunctional, and destructive.

Management

The Missional Denomination should provide *Conflict Management* services to its congregations when they have conflict situations that are at intensity four and in danger of escalating to five, before intensity five or six events occur. The hope is to intervene before the unhealthy conflict situation is so intense that nothing short of the direct, dramatic, and divine intervention of God, or the intervention of a third party from outside the denominational system and culture, will be enough to deal with it..

Such services, if possible, should be preceded by a *Conflict Ministry Assessment* that engages in the triage activities to determine the service that would best fit the need of the congregation. At times it may also be preceded by attempts at *Conflict Mediation*, but in the situations referred to above the mediation activities have apparently been insufficient to lower the intensity of conflict and it is actually continuing to rise.

The goal of the management aspect of this architecture is to provide intervention services to congregations that are focused on bringing in outside intervention to handle or manage the conflict situation so that the mission of the congregation can be redeemed from unhealthy, destructive, and dysfunctional ministry practice.

COACHING INSIGHTS

- What should be the role of denominations in the healthy and unhealthy conflict experienced by their affiliated congregations? Should it be a proactive role or a passive role? Describe the role you think would fit best.
- What is the responsibility of denominations to provide conflict awareness education, conflict resolutions services, and outside conflict mediation coaching and management consultation? Should these services be free to congregations, the cost shared, or the cost fully paid by the congregations?
- What has your denomination done to assist congregations in conflict situations? What is helpful? Unhelpful? Constructive? Destructive? Inadequate? Effective? What has gone right about it? What has gone wrong about it?
- Should a denomination support clergy in the midst of conflict situations or support the congregation? In what ways can it support both? What are the implications of how a denomination supports clergy and congregations in these situations?
- Should clergy and congregations be able to appeal any requirements made of them by the denomination, or by the coaches and consultants brought in by denominations to deal with conflict within the congregations? Describe how this appeal process should work.

PERSONAL REFLECTIONS

Your Reflections: What are your reflections on the material presented in this chapter?

_____

_____

_____

_____

_____

Your Actions: What actions do you need to take about your life, ministry, and/or denomination based on the material presented in this chapter?

_____

_____

_____

_____

_____

Your Accountability: How and by whom do you want to be held accountable for taking these actions?

_____

_____

_____

_____

_____

Afterword

EXECUTIVE SUMMARY

This Afterword contains some personal words for congregational lay leaders, staff members, pastors, and denominational staff persons. It is intended to encourage them to appropriately engage conflict as a strategy for congregational health and vision fulfillment.

An Afterword to Congregational Lay Leaders

Some years ago I was traveling through Missouri at night when my cell phone rang. A lay leader from a congregation on the East Coast was calling me on the advice of a denominational staff person who was also a member of the congregation. Their congregation was in conflict and needed some assistance.

A deacon in the congregation, member of the personnel team, and a good friend of the pastor, he called to gain understanding of the process of third-party conflict management and my possible interest in working with his congregation.

In his business life he did a lot of work with teams and their interaction. From his training he could clearly recognize that, unless his congregation engaged in a healthy process with an experienced facilitator, they were going to be in a lot of trouble.

This was the first of many conversations Trip and I had about his congregation. Ultimately, he was appointed chairperson of a team to recommend an outside third-party consultant. I became that consultant. Trip became chairperson of the team to work with me, and later he served on a strategic planning team when we moved beyond the immediate conflict situation and were able to build a new set of values, vision, and strategies for this congregation.

That was almost fifteen years ago. This congregation worked through its intensity five conflict, was able to set a new direction, call a new pastor, and continue to soar in quality and quantity. That pastor is still there, and no additional significant conflict situations have arisen in the life and ministry of the congregation. They have hardwired into their culture to revision their future every seven-to-nine years. They successfully went through a new round of revisioning a few years ago.

Trip was very helpful as a lay leader. Lay leaders such as Trip have the power to bless their congregations and be helpful. They also have the power to curse their congregations and be destructive. Further, various combinations of roles can be played out between these two polarities.

What role do you play in the life and ministry of your congregation when it comes to addressing conflict issues? Are you proactively able to engage conflict at a healthy intensity when it can be a positive ministry? Or, are you a carrier or even an antagonist who escalates conflict to the point it is unhealthy and destructive?

I pray healthy conflict ministry is your conviction and your practice.

An Afterword to Church Staff Members

A few years ago I was asked to coach a church staff—with emphasis on the associate pastor and the senior pastor—through a conflict situation. No one was quite sure how intense the conflict might be, but they knew it required outside assistance. The absence of a sense of team among the entire staff was the presenting issue. Concern was particularly expressed as to whether or not this senior pastor and associate pastor could work together.

Before my first visit to the congregation the spouse of the associate pastor called and asked me to participate in a ministry project in which they were engaged outside their local church ministry. It was a ministry that would provide me with some broader visibility that would be helpful to my ministry vocation as a strategic leadership coach.

It smelled fishy from the beginning. I would later discover I was right to reject this gracious offer, because there was a hook in it. It was an attempt to position me on the side of the associate pastor in the conflict situation. Who knows if it was intentional or not? All I know is I discovered a deeper pattern of manipulation that spoke to various dysfunctions.

In numerous other cases I have discovered staff ministers who are deeply loyal to their senior pastor and simultaneously to the congregation. They seek to support the senior pastor to the very limits of reasonable support and beyond when an unhealthy conflict situation arises. They also try to maintain perspective on the systems and processes of the congregation. Often these are situations in which staff ministers get caught in the middle.

This tendency for church staff persons to get caught in the middle of conflict makes your role in conflict a complicated role. How you play it out within the congregation is similar to lay leaders in that there is a lot of power to both bless and curse.

Among your best roles is the one that involves calling everyone to healthy process. Do not allow yourself to get caught in the middle between the senior pastor and the lay leadership. Do not criticize one to the other. Affirm what is right and build on it. Encourage lay leaders and the senior pastor to have genuine conversations with one another, and to pray without prejudice for the good of one another.

Realize criticism against you and pressure surrounding your job security may arise from at least two dynamics. First, as conflict escalates, the tendency to place everyone on one side or the other in the conflict includes you. Attempts will be made to make you declare where you are in the conflict rather than allowing you to serve all. You may not be able to remain neutral because you will be placed on one side or the other. But that does not mean your actions have to characterize those of the antagonists, be they actions by lay leaders or the senior pastor.

Second, when a conflict is heading for intensity five, in which attempts will be made to terminate the senior pastor, at times antagonists will test their ability to control the situation by seeing if they can terminate a staff person first. You need a support system around you within the congregation and outside the congregation that will allow you to retain perspective in the midst of assault.

I pray healthy conflict ministry is your conviction and your practice.

An Afterword to Church Pastors

Late one night a senior pastor, his personal coach, and myself were sitting in his office trying to discern appropriate next steps the pastor was willing to take in the midst of a highly intense conflict situation. The pastor had personal concerns regarding his ministry, his tenure at this congregation, and his worth and value as a minister. At the same time he had pastoral concerns he was trying to evaluate in the midst of this volatile situation.

His main antagonist was a person who had barely survived three heart attacks and various surgeries associated with them. The current rage of this lay leader caused the pastor to worry about this man's life. The pastor felt he had done everything he could to reconcile with this lay leader, and nothing was working.

A month later after attacking the pastor in a large group meeting, this lay leader exited the meeting in a rage, went home, and died of a massive heart attack. The pastor was right.

The most complex role in the midst of conflict belongs to the senior pastor. Pastors are in a unique position to know all the dynamics going on in their congregation. This creates a burden and extreme stress on senior pastors in the midst of complex conflict situations. It makes it hard for them to minister, deal with the conflict, and protect the integrity of their ministry at the same time. Too many pastors do not handle these dynamics well, but fall into unhealthy patterns that aggravate the conflict situation.

Senior pastors can do several things to proactively lead congregations through complex conflict situations. First, they can initiate conflict ministry education in their congregations to teach all leaders a common language and approach to conflict situations. Second, they can practice personally, and lead staff and lay leaders to practice, the learnings from their conflict ministry education.

Third, pastors can maintain an active and healthy spiritual life, and have various ministry colleagues and other friends who are personal support and accountability persons to them. These actions will empower pastors to maintain spiritual and leadership perspective on the complex issues facing their congregations.

Fourth, pastors can call on all their available resources to keep from unnecessarily escalating conflict situations. Pastors are seldom the original cause of unhealthy conflict. But they are the number one person to escalate conflict when it reaches a point at which they feel personally threatened by it.

Fifth, fight the tendency to marginalize your accusers and declare them to be unreasonable and uncontrollable antagonists. Some people may become this, but generally not as many as you think, and not as quickly as you think.

Remember you have the greatest ability in the congregation to bless or curse the congregational community. No one has the opportunity you have to speak to the active congregation corporately on a weekly basis, and personally on a regular basis. Use those times wisely. Do not abuse those times.

I pray healthy conflict ministry is your conviction and your practice.

An Afterword to Denominational Staff Persons

Some years ago I spent a day with a denominational staff to help them think through why the incidents of conflict were continuing to increase in their affiliated congregations at the same time efforts of their staff to help congregations deal with conflict had significantly increased.

A few years earlier each of the five program staff persons had taken training on various approaches to conflict resolution, mediation, and management. They had then offered their services to their congregations. Rather than helping to diminish conflict situations, this move had increased the number of conflict situations. Why?

In telling congregations the staff had become experts in various approaches to conflict situations, they "enticed" the congregations to find ways to label whatever was going on with them as conflict. They found ways to positively answer the question the staff was asking, which was: "Do you have any conflict in your church?"

While conflict ministry needs to be part of the portfolio of services offered or brokered by your denominational organizations, it does not need to be a lead service. You should lead with those services that empower the mission, purpose, and vision of congregations.

You can fix all the problems in all your congregations and still only bring them right up to neutral. It is what is right about your congregations that should form the basis of future ministry. What are they called by God to do to enhance the kingdom of God? Dealing with this question with your congregations will empower them long-term to deal with conflict better than asking them if they have conflict. In spite of what you think, they basically like you and will try to answer the questions you ask. Be careful what questions you ask them.

Be the provider of conflict ministry education and the broker of conflict management services by outside third parties. This will give you the opportunity to be seen as persons who help congregations with really great ministry, but also brokers of the services for those times when the congregation is stuck.

I pray healthy conflict ministry is your conviction and practice.

An Afterword for the Entire Congregation

A couple of years ago my wife and I moved back to Columbia, South Carolina, where we had lived seventeen years previously. We had raised our children here. We had loved our church here. And we had our best friends here.

We purchased the house of a church friend that had an in-ground pool. That was a bonus. I would probably never spend the money on installing a pool in my backyard. Since this house came with a pool, it is very nice to have it.

I have thought back to when I was young and how I learned to swim. My older sisters and my parents tried to teach me. Stubborn even when I was young, I learned to swim underwater first, and then to do a dog paddle. My front crawl swimming stroke was nothing to emulate. I was actually ten years old before I took lessons and learned proper technique. Then in high school I took additional swimming lessons at school.

I ultimately learned everything I needed to known to enjoy swimming for my life. It would never have occurred to me to swim in pools, lakes, and oceans without knowing something about how to swim.

In the same way, congregations need to learn how to swim through the diverse currents of conflict that are encountered at different times in various ways in congregations. Without conflict ministry education, congregations are likely to drown because they cannot swim in the midst of conflict.

Why then does it not occur to congregations they need to learn—together, if possible—something about the conflict ministry process that will be helpful to their life and ministry? Over the next year, make this a goal of your congregation.

Lay leadership, staff ministers, and the senior pastor need to engage in conflict ministry education together. This will assist in developing a conflict ministry culture in your congregation through which you can deal with typical conflict of everyday congregation life. In addition, you can hardwire into your congregational culture how you will deal with the inevitable unhealthy conflict when it occurs.

The proclamation of the love of the Triune God, the worship of the Triune God, and living in a Christ-centered, faith-based community with one another are of sufficient importance that you need to inoculate your culture against the intervention of the Evil One. "Put on the whole armor of God, so that you will be able to stand firm against the schemes of the devil" (Eph. 6:11).

I pray healthy conflict ministry is your conviction and your practice.

PERSONAL REFLECTIONS

Your Reflections: What are your reflections on the material presented in this afterword?

Your Actions: What actions do you need to take about your life, ministry, and/or congregation based on the material presented in this afterword?

Your Accountability: How and by whom do you want to be held accountable for taking these actions?

Christ-Centered Coaching
7 Benefits for Ministry Leaders
BY JANE CRESWELL

"Coach Jane Creswell is the consummate leader in bringing coaching principles to life in a church or organization. Her words of wisdom will impact your organization more than you can imagine."

■ Laurie Beth Jones, author of *Jesus, CEO; The Path;* and *Jesus, Life Coach*

978-08272-04997

Recreating the Church
Leadership for the Postmodern Age
BY RICHARD L. HAMM

"Dick Hamm asks an essential—and deeply faithful—question of the church: Where are we going? Then, through analysis and insight into both past and future, and with an unwavering commitment to the mission of the church, Hamm points us in the right directions."

■ Wesley Granberg-Michaelson, General Secretary, Reformed Church in America

978-08272-32532

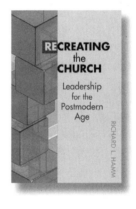

Pursuing the Full Kingdom Potential of Your Congregation
BY GEORGE W. BULLARD JR.

"If you want your church to mature and get beyond the preservation stage and to fulfill God's will for Kingdom growth, then study, read, and pray through this book."

■ Denton Lotz, General Secretary, Baptist World Alliance

978-08272-29846

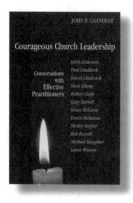

Courageous Church Leadership
Conversations with Effective Practitioners
BY JOHN P. CHANDLER

"Great leadership hinges primarily on one thing—finding the courage to be yourself. Chandler uncovers the stories of some who found that courage and became remarkable leaders."

▪ Jim Henderson, executive director of Off-the-Map, former director of leadership development at Vineyard Community Church

978-08272-05062

The Heart of the Matter
Changing the World God's Way
BY CHARLES HALLEY

"With great insight and real world testing, Charlie Halley points out that personal transformation and congregational transformation are inseparable."

▪ Don Cousins, congregational coach, former executive director of Willow Creek Community Church

978-08272-14521

Enduring Connections
Creating a Preschool and Children's Ministry
BY JANICE HAYWOOD

Providing a thorough introduction to preschool and children's ministries, Janice Haywood addresses the questions a childhood minister faces and ways to answer them.

978-08272-08216